Peace Within

HOW I DEVELOPED
A RELATIONSHIP
WITH NATURE

Peace Within: How I Developed a Relationship with Nature
Copyright © 2025 by John Cole

All rights reserved. No part of this book may be used or reproduced in any form, electronic or mechanical, including photocopying, recording, or scanning into any information storage and retrieval system, without written permission from the author except in the case of brief quotation embodied in critical articles and reviews.

Front cover, About the Author, and My Heartfelt Conclusion pictures provided by the author (taken in Jamaica, Vermont). Image for Chapter 10 from Shutterstock.com, all other images from 123RF.com

Book design by The Troy Book Makers
Printed in the United States of America
The Troy Book Makers • Schodack Landing, New York • thetroybookmakers.com

To order additional copies of this title,
contact your favorite local bookstore
or visit www.shoptbmbooks.com

ISBN: 978-1-61468-984-3

Peace Within

HOW I DEVELOPED
A RELATIONSHIP
WITH NATURE

JOHN COLE

Peace Within
is lovingly dedicated
to my Mother and Father.
Your time and devotion
taught me many things.
Beginning at age three,
and our bedside prayers.
Thank you.

Foreword

I am sixty seven years old. Approximately twenty five years ago, I realized that someday I would be writing this book. I am now retired. A nature loving person throughout my entire life, I am an everyday person confronted with the same issues, more or less, as you, every day. Although I am not Native American, I would call myself a deeply religious and spiritual man starting with a very strong connection to Nature. Enjoy your read.

I am thankful for my family, Mom and Dad, and Todd, and John and Katherine, and Kaden.

I am thankful for my friends and all relationships that have played a role in my life and I in yours.

I am thankful for my relationship with Nature.

I am thankful for the opportunity to share my understanding of Nature with you, the reader, and the comfort and happiness it may bring.

I am thankful for the permissions granted by the quoted authors and publishers in my book.

A special acknowledgement to The Troy Book Makers for their time and energy in getting this published book to you, the reader.

A very special thanks to my spiritual teachers who came into my life and continue to support me with their essence and presence.

I am always thankful for faith and spirit.

I recognize that one of the most valuable things in life, is a time a parent gives you or you a parent, or as a parent, your presence.

This book is dedicated to you, Mom and Dad. Thank you.

Contents

Foreword vii

Introduction 1

Chapter 1: My First Vision - My Day Begins 3

Chapter 2: Developing A Relationship With Nature 27

Chapter 3: Seeing Animals in Nature 55

Chapter 4: Eagle Speaks to Me 67

Chapter 5: Recognizing the elements 79

Chapter 6: Recognizing Energy 89

Chapter 7: Power of Place 103

Chapter 8: The Cave 115

Chapter 9: The Cabin 125

Chapter 10: Enhancing your Relationship with Nature 135

Chapter 11: The Call from the Spirits 147

Chapter 12: Counting My Blessings 151

My Heartfelt Conclusion 155

Recommended Readings 157

Bibliography 161

About the Author 165

Introduction

Nature has taught me many things. Walks in Nature calm my body, release my stresses, and clears my mind. More importantly, I am in the moment, enjoying each step, my attention focused on myself and Nature. The open air and the sunshine. The rivers, mountains and waterfalls. The season's changing colors. Winter's first snow fall. Flying eagles. Bounding deer. Dancing stars. Thoughts often influence our quality of life and I am happy most when I am in Nature.

Nature remains an orderly and meaningful place in my life. My relationship with Nature has opened up many spiritual realms for me. It is a relationship that will only grow stronger. It is a relationship that will never be taken away from me. Nature allows me to focus on the truth and man's relationship to all things. I respect all spiritual paths and many do in fact, exist. Each life has a sacred path. Discover who you are. Make peace with yourself and others. And most importantly, Peace Within.

I will begin by writing about the day that I learned that I might be losing my job and how Nature opened up to me at a time of need. I went to a familiar place in Nature, a place I had walked many times to calm my body, clear my mind and be present.

The second chapter will describe how I developed a relationship with Nature over time, physically, mentally, emotionally and spiritually.

Subsequent chapters describe some of my special experiences. Talking with eagles… rivers and mountains….spiritual experiences…. the cave…. and the cabin where much of my writing takes place.

Intermittently and respectively, chapters will show you how I recognize animals in Nature, recognize the elements in Nature, recognize energy in Nature, and finding your special place in Nature (power of place).

Chapter 10 will provide you with ways to enhance your relationship with Nature.

Chapter 11 describes one of my special spiritual experiences.

Lastly, in Chapter 12 I will share what the spiritual essence of Nature has done for me and can do for you.

It was my intention to wait one year into retirement to publish this book. I wrote this book years ago and now I am retired and my live has evolved almost full circle from home to cave to cabin to home ….things have obviously changed for the better. We carry the knowledge we have learned with us. Now, still is the time for me to share with you. Discover who you are and make peace with yourself and others. And most importantly, **Peace within.**

Chapter 1

My First Vision
My Day Begins

It has been said that as we walk, all of our ancestors walk with us. So one should not be surprised that we might see one.

On November 14, 1995. My dramatic day begins when I receive formal notice from my employer that I was being furloughed from my job. Meaning don't come back to work until we tell you. This happened because the Government had not passed a budget to fund the federal agencies. The furlough was expected to last anytime up to thirty days.

I was informed to leave by 1PM that afternoon and left before that. I was making $2000 a month, paying child support, a mortgage, taxes. Living pay check to pay check. Watch how I spend money. No pay check. What if I'm out of work for a week? Two weeks? Four weeks? Divorced a few years, single, bills to pay. No immediate family in the area.

Where was I to turn?

What was I to do?

Today. I chose to walk a familiar path at Jamaica State Park. I had walked this trail over one hundred times the past few years. And its repetitive nature and beauty enhanced my experiences that much more. At times, I would be drawn here, like today. Jamaica State Park, closes for the season around Columbus Day weekend. A brochure describes the "West River Trail as one of few converted rail beds in southern Vermont, the section in the park is universally-accessible and great for easy walking, jogging or biking. The trail meanders along the West River, following the old bed of the West River Railroad." I had truly developed a relationship with Jamaica State Park.

I called friends, only message machines answered. No friends. No work. No money. Everyone else has a job and is working. I'm alone.

It began to snow lightly as I leave my Keene, New Hampshire work place and drive twenty miles to my Brattleboro, Vermont home. I was excited to see the first snow fall and ready to walk in it. Part of me wanted to walk and part of me wanted that friend to talk with. I'm alone. All I could think about on my ride home were my life circumstances and getting in touch with a friend. I'll get home, try calling a few friends, get dressed and go.

Thirty minutes later, I'm home. I walk through my back door towards my family room phone. Check my answering machine, no messages. I call my friends a few more times. "You've reached so so, I'm not able to come to the phone right now, please leave a message and I'll call you back as soon as I can...."

how I developed a relationship with nature

Still alone, still anxious to walk, like a child waiting to go outside in the season's first snowfall. I change into layers of clothing, a hiking parka, my hiking boots, and gloves. My back pack filled with a large bottle of water, power bars, granola bars, flash lights, an extra pair of socks and gloves, an aluminum blanket, matches and my bright red bandanas. Home but maybe ten minutes, I'm ready to go. I am determined to walk a path that was part of my growing relationship with Nature.

Anticipation and excitement grows as I make my 30 minute drive down Route 30, a single lane highway with trees near roadside and mountain views, left and right and front on, glimpses of the river at times. I'm driving in rural country to the small village of Jamaica Vermont. Again, the Jamaica State Park brochure describes that for thousands of years, Native Americans traveled the West River by canoe, following a major transportation route between the Connecticut River and Lake Champlain. Abundant food sources, especially salmon, were attractive to the native inhabitants. A major archaeological dig unearthed a large Abenaki campsite on the banks of the Salmon Hole. Evidence suggests that the present day Jamaica village area was a center for hunting, fishing, plant gathering and tool making for a period of over 8000 years.

I'm driving as if a part of me was waiting there for me. Like going to meet your girl friend or wife after a long day to share the day's events or visit your young child missing them, going to and finding that comforting place. This was quite the place for many Native American tribes many years ago, two intersecting waterways, the mountains, the streams running into the upper west river, flat land, trees. And quite the place for me in my years as well.

Are we there yet? I am going to my place. When you're half way there, you are half way there. I am following the river as I drive along Route 30 just as the Native Americans paddled on the river. Mountains to my left, mountains straight ahead, mountains to my right. Barren trees, pine trees, and more trees. Very few homes. This is Vermont.

I finally arrive in the town of Jamaica, Vermont and turn onto Depot Street over a bridge that crosses over the Ball Mountain brook. This waterway flows east into the West River about a half mile below Jamaica State Park.

A few minutes later, I approach a one lane, green iron bridge which frames in the entry into the natural world of Jamaica State Park.

D-bunk, d-bunk, d-bunk as I drive slowly over the pair of vertical parallel planks that strike against the underlying horizontal ones. I always pause in the middle of the bridge with my near car window down. I look north through an assortment of green beams and rails and I see the mountains and tree lines on each side of the West River. Fifteen feet of shoreline on each side, mostly tall grasses on the west side, and less to my right. Snowflakes fall and disappear into the rapids. It is here, in this glacier carved valley that I can see the energy spread above and across the fast approaching waters.

I continue driving about 50 yards and turn left onto a private road - Salmon Hole Lane and park next to a large brown sign with yellow lettering that reads Jamaica State Park Camping Hiking Picnicking.

I exit my car, strap on my back pack and walk about 50 feet towards the closed large brown gates that close the traffic to the park. Its about thirty degrees or less, an overcast sky, snow still falling, just covering the ground. As I pass by a small opening to my left, I feel my boots sink into a thick carpet of pine needles. I'm finally here. Like walking through the front door. Honey, I'm home. Getting hugged by my children. Nature is my stable partner.

Entering the Park-Initial Path

This is a truly remarkable landscape. The ground and trails, the trees and forest, the streams running into the river, the cliffs and ledges by your side, and the mountains reaching to the sky. I have walked this path many, many times, in all seasons and in all weather. I thought I had seen it all. This day is no different, or would it be? Excited to be here.

Snowing before Thanksgiving. How often does that happen?

Stepping on pine needles, layers of pine needles, interconnected in an intimate way. I walk towards the river a few steps and bare to my right. I see and hear the rapids to my left. The view of the river is partially obscured by the tall pines, it demands my attention still even though the main park entrance and its driveway remain in full sight to the right.

A hundred paces further, I enter a canopy, mostly hemlock. Some branches hang as low as six feet from the ground. A lot of saplings, primarily hemlock, some mixed hardwoods appear on both sides of me.

My path is about twenty feet wide, made up of primarily pine needles. Its a half mile long and a little bit more forgiving than the last lay of pine needles. The pine needles and underlying roots are connected in such a way that I sink less but spring more in my step.

I smell the hemlock - smells like strong scented Christmas candles.

I am surrounded by trees. The gray sky and snowflakes squeeze through the heavy canopy above. Oak and beech leaves surround the base of their respective trees to my right. Small twigs lay on the ground. I cannot put my arms around the mighty hemlocks to my left and right. They stand three feet wide and some eighty feet tall, extending their branches over the river bed. Fewer beech branches hang there as well.

I hear birds chirping.

I see small birds hiding and flying amongst the branches as if they are playing hide and seek and allowing themselves to be seen only this one time.

I feel close to the river on my left. The bank descends abruptly between ten to twenty feet along the way.

I still hear the river. Sometimes, loud rapids. Other times, quiet tranquil waters. Intermittently, every fifty or hundred feet, rapids, still waters, rapids, still waters….

To my right, there is long row of leantos that face the river. They are spaced seventy-five feet apart. Round iron grill pits and picnic tables lie in front each structure. Man's creations. I feel exposed as each driveway creates an opening to the main park road each time I walk by a lean-to. I can feel a cold breeze at these openings. I'm not aware of the created distraction at this time.

Just before the final and seventh lean-to, I notice a long island in the middle of the river. A set of rapids, perhaps ten feet wide, separate it from the shoreline. The island extends maybe two hundred feet and is fifteen to fifty wide at times. Its composed of smaller trees, mainly tall grasses and brush. I can see past the vegetation to the other side of the river and its rapids there.

I listen closely and I can hear the water on both sides of island, separately, the near rapids and the distant rapids. Here and now. Just as you can hear people talking at the same time.

The path narrows as I come upon a nature center with a large covered pavilion area. Picnic tables lie on a cement floor. A gathering place for young and old nature explorers when the park is open.

Next, I walk up and down a small gully and come upon the park's bathrooms. The second parking lot is to my immediate right.

I'm in the open.

The snow falls directly on me.

I feel the cold air against my face. No breeze, just cold air.

Only a few steps away, lies a path down to the river to a spot called the Salmon Hole. Two mighty oak stand at the head of this trail, one on each side. Salmon Hole is a popular swimming area but long ago, some thirty tribes lived here. It was their home. "They often lived at a physically attractive spot for settlement or a temporary camp. Many times a seasonal spot although elders often remained. The sites were chosen for their advantages: an elevation with a pleasing view, yet defensible. A place always protected by the north wind by a hill or evergreens. A clear, flowing spring. A source of firewood nearby. Close to the water - a sea, a river, one or more lakes where fishing was good. Two or three streams into river provided food and easy travel. Nearby light land that could be cleared for planting. Salmon for food and for fertilizing." (1) This was one of those spots. An unlimited amount of salmon in this part of the river. Thus, the name Salmon Hole.

I continue to walk alongside the river, fully exposed to my right, rather than walk more directly across the parking lot to the next river path.

There's always sparse grass in this area despite the park's attempt to seed the ground here. Too much foot traffic or acidic hemlock perhaps.

Picnic tables are turned on their sides (as the park is now closed) and the charcoal standing grills remain intact and fastened to the ground.

I still hear the river. The rapids can sound like oncoming crashing waves in the ocean, only from a distance.

I see no one.

There is no confusion. No uncertainty.

My mind already clear.

I really enjoy my walks here . Its a long, level, winding path that follows the West river and nearby mountains. This is where it all comes together. I belong here.

I'm not influenced by the fear based forces we face in society. Society, technology, and the furlough are quickly behind me.

I am here and now.

The river rapids have slowed and are distant.

My attention is here and now.

All is quiet.

Tom Brown describes it best, "There is no separation of Nature and spirit. Nature becomes a door way to spirit and spirit becomes a door way to Nature. There is only the sacred oneness that we are all part of stepping in that door. " (2)

I am about to step in. Thank you.

Familiar Path

I can still hear the river faintly as I enter the river path to my left.

This winding path is a walk in the park. The path remains somewhat level and you never feel as if you're climbing or exerting yourself. It's a relaxing walk for all ages to experience.

Again, having walked here many times, a relationship has been formed here, away from modern society. I was growing at alarming rate and accepted my responsibility that came with our new beginnings and experiences. An awareness and mindfulness followed our familiarity as I tuned in to my surroundings with my senses.

Generally, you will always see the river on this portion of the path.

Along the way, a few paths will lead down to the water at times, mostly steep, some 45 degrees or less.

The sun does not shine on this path, usually over the river and to the west side far side.

As soon as you walk in, I immediately notice a second canopy of tree limbs and branches overhead, however, this time of year you also see quite a bit of sky as the leaves have fallen. This canopy consists of primarily hardwoods and is higher than before.

I see a lot of snowflakes. No two snowflakes alike. They fall across, laterally vertically no special direction up and down swirling sideways slow fast floating falling blending into the environment to complete a black and white portrait.

There are four camp sites to my right just as I begin to walk away from the river for a short distance. Then trees appear on my immediate left and right. Moss generally climbs all trees to a foot above the ground. Moss covered rocks as well, of many sizes.

Initially, its quiet here. The shoreline widens between fifty to seventy-five feet at times. The massive hemlocks soon disappear from the shoreline and are replaced by the taller hardwoods and the smaller hemlock. Big boulders appear closer to shore.

I can feel the breeze here against my face and hands as I am not sheltered by the mighty hemlocks. The trees are the same height here but of a smaller diameter, perhaps a foot.

The center of the path is obviously more traveled and worn and of gritty sandy gravel. I generally walk left, closer to the river, closer to the mountain views and closer to the softer earth. Meaning more decomposed leaves and pine needles tend to accumulate on the sides of the path and I feel my steps into the earth below me.

Walking comfortably.

When you look left you will see the river as it changes between its rapids and its flat water. The sound and flow of the river can change every one hundred feet. Mostly hardwoods and smaller hemlocks line the river edge. Leaves have fallen, creating an opening for us to appreciate this alternating pattern in Nature.

I can see the trees and the mountainside across the river as well.

When you look right the landscape becomes hilly and will generally remain so on this path. Big rocks, pine needles, trees, limbs, branches and leaves of all stages of decay lay on the ground. Partially decayed white birch logs and bark stand out. Fallen trees usually hemlock, some hardwoods. Moss green covered rocks laying against the darker leaves on the ground. Ferns dispersed alongside the path.

I am surrounded by forest everywhere.

The descent to the river on my left is steep, twenty-five to thirty feet, anywhere from forty-five to ninety degrees.

The ascent to the hills on my right can generally be seen for anywhere up to one hundred feet and in some instances can climb up to sixty degrees.

Two hundred paces later, I appear to be under a canopy much like a tunnel. Not the first time, not the last. Big rocks appear to my right as far as 30 feet in from the path. Long branches cross over above me.

Small four to six foot pine trees are on my left. I stand closely by them and watch as a their branches move ever so slightly - an inch each way. I watch as a bead of water drops off a branch.

I touch their newly formed soft lime colored needles. I appreciate their feel. I acknowledge it. I am thankful for the moment.

Snow falling.

Chipmunks are moving and talking and peering at me from behind trees, rocks and leaves, and holes in the ground.

At times, ledge will appear on my right, ascending enough that I am not climbing it and the land to my left, descending enough that I am sliding down it if I ever want to meet the river.

Eventually, I come upon an opening in the shoreline where a gradual wide path leads down to a sandy/rock laden beach.

When you look up you will see the mountain across the river.

The cliffs are some three hundred feet high above the river. Some massive hemlocks will rise above them yet and above the hardwoods tree line by fifty feet.

Long ago, The Native Americans would retreat to the safety of this mountain and its caves. I would later explore this mountain, its many trails and find myself abruptly facing this very view below, backtracking my steps to my own safety. Nothing ventured, nothing gained. Through time and my perseverance, I did find the caves and hidden places of protection where for years to come, I would meditate year round. (more on that in Chapter 8).

I continue walking.

To my right, I hear song birds one last time.

Huge hemlocks appear again on each side of me for say forty feet before the path then widens to forty feet.

The river bends significantly right and the path narrows and ascends slightly, following the river. Trees have fallen to my right. While sparse trees appear on the shoreline and the descent is a drastic thirty feet down to the river. Steep, steep ledge beginning at 30 feet tall continue for two hundred feet on my right. Green moss covers most of the ledge and dripping water falls from it at times. This is the first vortex on this river path. There is little room here as you face the vast openness of river and valley and high ledges behind you. As I turn, I can hear the oncoming rapids to my left and the same on my right as well as the sound deflects off of the ledge. There is some shoreline here, twenty-five feet perhaps, so the water does not appear right on top of you.

What is a vortex? A vortex is a high energy area. Most people think of the center of a tornado when they hear the word vortex.

Jaap Van Etten PHD further describes a vortex as a place where vibrational essences serve as portals or doorways, to help you directly connect with a particular being, object, or place... The essence of a vortex can also be caught by water. (3) More on this topic as we move further along.

Looking ahead. I'm about to enter another canopy in front of me. Green appears on both sides, white in the ground and sky.

To my right, I see those few, tan leaves that remain attached to the beech trees, and I can hear them bristling in the wind.

An overlook trail appears on my right at times. It parallels this path at about twenty feet above it, overlooking us and meandering through the forest as well.

I stay on the course of the river path.

I rest and face the river at times. The river this day is flowing as it normally flows. Not rushing like a day after a storm. Flowing naturally. The water is normally clear. Rocks, big and small lay above and below its surface. Their colors contrast between white, gray, brown and light brown. The river is wide , there are rapids on the near side and slow moving water on the far side, movement and stillness in one place. Both present.

Moving on.

I also see beaver cut logs at rivers edge occasionally as one beaver can be seen swimming nearby as well.

Long branches, twigs of hardwoods usually lie on right side of the path.

The decaying leaves and still water have an organic smell to them.

A bit further, having walked about a mile now, I arrive at the "dumplings". Named for its large boulders that were dumped here in the river from the glaciers many years ago. This a popular white water spot for kayakers as there is no escaping it, you must enter through its fast and exit through its faster openings. Fast moving rapids in and out, one hundred feet above and below the dumplings. The river narrows here as well, forty feet. The boulders form a circle where water enters and exits fast thru the middle and sides of the circle. With it and in it, energy moves swirling up and down in whirl pools. There are four openings in each circle, each a foot or two wide. I can see the white as the water runs around and away from the rocks. The boulders are immense, some twenty feet wide and long and fifteen feet above the current water levels. Across the river more ledge along the mountainside. A steep twenty foot lateral path leads you down to the river. Its loud and fast. Always the perfect spot to stop and let your emotions go in the fast moving rapids.

The riverside has sparse growth, only small hemlock and hardwoods.

Behind me, bubbles follow each other in a straight line of ripples as the water flows south. And further, its white suds stream along for about 200 feet as far as you can see down the river.

I perceive another opening to a canopy ahead of me. Both sides green and lined with hemlocks.

Large ash, grey birch, a few oak trees, and mostly hemlock obscure a beach on my left. Below lies the most tranquil spot on the river. I follow a narrow, side bending, manageable forty-five degree path to the river.

It seems like the water collects here as if a beaver dam blocks the flow of water any further down stream, but not. Ledge across the river climbs up the mountain yet again. One hundred feet of still water is up and down from you. This is truly a place to calm my body, calm my mind, and calm my emotions. Many times have been spent here, sitting and meditating on healing thoughts.

Always at a better place upon leaving, I ascend to a small grove of fifteen foot pines that surround a picnic table to my left. Even closer to and partially visible to the path. I would often lie here, rest and relax, close my eyes, and listen to nothing. Although just a picnic table, it feels like you're lying in comfort on a stiff mattress. And I would venture on, more at peace than before.

As I leave I smell the hemlock again as if strong scented Christmas candles are burning.

My confusion and uncertainty has long disappeared.

how I developed a relationship with nature

My Favorite Place

A few hundred steps further, I come upon my favorite bend in the river that I will call the second vortex. The path and river significantly bear left in front of me. The path narrows and slightly ascends to a fifty foot plateau.

I feel the breeze of cold air.

The initial ledge begins at twenty-five feet to as high as 75 feet. Water drops off the moss covered ledge on my right and no shoreline exists below me on my left. The path might be twelve feet wide and descends vertically twenty-five feet to the river. Fewer trees exist on the ledge side but there are enough from both sides of the path to maintain the canopy above me.

Moss creeps in from both the waters edge and the path ledge.

Mountains to my east, west and north and densely populated hemlocks in all directions enclose this space. Yet everything appears expansive when you look away from this small place.

I look across at the river. The river just comes at you here. Water enters this area from streams on both sides of the river. Whirlpools then swirl amongst the rocks and the rushing water form the oncoming rapids.

The river rushes into this spot and veers off in another direction while the cooler breeze, sound and energy is left to bounce off the ledge behind me and whomever is in is path. And for those aware of it, the energy may flow through you.

My ear towards the river, hears the river. My ear away from the river, hears the river, as a reflection off the ledge. Much like hearing a car behind you on a busy street, you hear several cars approaching you. The sound can be enhanced when wearing a hood as I was this day (like a sea shell hears the ocean, I heard the oncoming rapids)

This location will appear to be much different than the first vortex as Jaap Van Etten continues to describe a vortex as an area where you can feel the ancestral energies of the people who lived here before us and can communicate with us while we are in a certain state of consciousness ....(4) And I was not surprised to learn from others while I was completing research for this book that this river and the surrounding forest and mountains are energetic areas of spiritual encounters. Again, I'll share more as I walk further along my path.

Quiet Path

As I walk away from the second vortex, my wonder turns to thankfulness. My favorite mountain stream appears fifty paces on my right. I always stop here, walk upstream some, kneel down, cup some cold water with my hand, always cold water, and splash it over my forehead. A cleansing. A baptism of sorts. A true expression of my gratitude, renewing my honor and respect for mother earth. Touching water. I'm here. I'm glad to be here.

I continue north. Snow falling.

The shoreline increases to seventy-five feet from the river.

The slope at 60 degrees with a rocky moss earth covers the hillside to my right for one hundred feet. Sporadic trees. I could walk up the side on all fours to a clearing on top to explore (and have but not this day).

I come upon the grayish birch trees 2 to 3 feet apart and 6 inch diameter. I always stop here and hug them. I put one of my arms around one and another arm around the other. I close my eyes. I meditate a few minutes. Its like leaning into your slow dancing partner. I feel special and connected to my partner/tree. I feel the energy and the vibration of the earth coming up through me.

I have spent a lot of time here. I walked this path many times during the spring, summer, fall and winter. Whether it was sunny or cloudy, raining and snowing, hot or cold. I developed a relationship with this place. Thus, as I stated earlier Nature has become my stable partner.

how I developed a relationship with nature

Two dozen hemlocks appear on my left and continue to lead me away from the river. They stand one hundred feet tall and three feet wide. The canopy grows taller alongside it.

Ferns, seedlings at times on each side of path.

Touching the snow. I remove my gloves and hat and feel the snow landing on me.

Access to an overlook path appears on my right. I have only walked it a handful times because I enjoy the repeated landscape of the river path. It seems to enhance my experience tenfold much like a repeated mantra in a meditative way. While the overlook path is narrow, less traveled, more open to the adjacent forest, and further from the river.

Speaking of the river, I don't hear it as much.

Tuning in, tuning out. Seeing and hearing and smelling according to the landscape as it changes repeatedly in front of you. Seeing and hearing the rapids, you are drawn to the river, focus is there.

My attention and focus now turns to the forest, mountains and sky and the path in front of me. I look ahead. I'm looking more and more. I have a heightened awareness to my surroundings. Everything appears closer. More prominent in the distance and have a presence. They seem to jump out at me and demand attention. Wow wow.

More and more I appreciate everything.

Everything is special here. Sacred.

I am aware of the silence.

No thought. No worries. No distractions. Clearly appreciative of the moment and setting. I constantly acknowledge my surroundings. I give thanks to my surroundings and this moment.

Snow falling steadily as I walk on.

I come across the intermittent changes in the landscapes once again. An overlook trail to my right. The slow moving river to my left. Still, silence. Forest on my right. A canopy here. A canopy there. All the while, expanding my consciousness and well being in this place and time.

The landscape is more accessible on both sides of the path. Fifty to hundred feet of wooded shoreline on my left and forest and streams to my right. Pooled water remains on both sides of the path.

Learning Path

I disappear into the forest as I enter the longest canopy on this path. It looks like a tunnel before me but it seems more like a rite of passage based upon my journey and frame of mind so far. I'm lead further away from the river. It lasts for at least one hundred yards (the length of a football field). Yes, I continue to see things. To my right, a waterfall stream that I visit quite frequently but would only acknowledge this time as I walk by it and a side trail to Hamilton Falls that lies just before reaching my destination, Cobb brook.

But more importantly, I notice things I didn't notice before.

I look up and I begin to understand how the canopy can change on the path based upon the height and proximity of the trees to the path. Younger trees, oak, maple, beech have tendency to have branches over lay the path. Some large hemlock not often. The lower and smaller canopies have the younger trees and saplings. Mixture of hardwoods young and old make diverse canopies. 2 to 3 inch saplings curve over at 20 feet. Taller ones go vertical and branch out over the path. Older trees go vertical or lean or branch over to reach the sunlight, yet higher.

I begin to realize just how many times I have walked through these varying canopies this day and yet how similar they appear before me each time. Present space. Open. Present space. Closed. Again, Tom Brown describes it best, "Nature becomes a door way to spirit and spirit becomes a door way to Nature. There is only the sacred oneness that we are all part of stepping in that door." (2)

I had no concept of distance and time in this moment. I was just moving along and enjoying the moment and in retrospect, learning a few things along the way.

Lastly, I'm slowly losing my senses and becoming a part of my surroundings. My awareness, my being, my energy focused upon Nature's oneness, all relations. Eventually merging as one.

My Meditative Place

Up ahead, my path widens and the canopy opens up once again. It is here that Cobb Brook runs into the West River. I call this a vortex area as well. I normally rest and meditate here and today would be no different. I remove my back pack and sit on the park bench, placing my back pack beside me. I am sitting about thirty to forty feet above the river. A tree to my left and a tree to my right frame in the picture perfectly. I see snowflakes falling from all directions in the sky, here I can tell that there are no two alike.

I grab a bottle of water and a power bar from my back pack. First the water, I can feel the cold water flowing from my mouth down my throat, a soothing cold, through my chest, a cool feeling, to my stomach, cold. Second the power bar, I feel it nourishing my entire body, bringing strength to arms, body and legs. More water. More nourishment.

All the while, I'm looking at the winter wonderland in front of me. We have a very highly charged area where the brook and river connect with its respective flowing waters and energies. We have mountains, higher than ever before on this path. Mountains to our left and mountains to our right. The Ball Mountain Dam sits one quarter mile up the river, hidden from view by landscape. The dam stands 265 feet high and 915 feet long, holding back almost eighteen billion gallons of water for flood control purposes. Yet permitting a consistent flow of water year round.

All waters and energy are funneled into this space. To me this is the most charged area on this path. Actually, one of the most charged areas I have ever been, secluded in Nature. Yet I always become grounded and balanced here. Initially, this was my favorite place in Nature, a place I was attracted to, a place that feels good. (5) Now this is vortex.

I partially unzip my parker and remove my separate hood. I can see the steam leaving the top of my head. For now, I have a warm body and more than happy to remove a layer of clothing and my gloves.

I gaze back over the river, visualizing the vibration energy coming off the water. Yes, I can see the energy. It looks something like the heat rising off the hot summer pavement or the electrical energy rising above the power lines at times. Or better yet, it closely resembles the fuzzy screens on the old black and white television sets, only not as fuzzy?

Energy. I welcome that energy into my body. I lean forward and stand in front of the park bench. I close my eyes. I motion it towards me by extending my arms out slowly, palms pushing away, and curling my arms back towards my chest slowly, palms facing me. Four more postures follow. (I'll describe this meditation fully in Chapter 10) . I repeat this action several more times, slowly and deliberately. Reciting my personal mantra all the while. A prayer. I open my eyes when I can feel the tingling of energy in my fingertips and the sensation throughout my entire body, from head to toe. My crown chakra is open. I feel balanced. I am now totally relaxed. My energy and mind in a good place. Very far from man made inventions. In Nature.

Next, I walk about fifteen paces down a slope to my right to Cobb Brook. Cobb Brook is the water source for one of tallest waterfalls in Vermont. Hamilton Falls is 125 feet high. Water continues to flow down the mountain from these falls. The brook can be steep at times and difficult to traverse as it too, seems carved into the mountainside. The water flows rapidly into the West River. I kneel down and cup my hand in the moving water. Just enough to wet my forehead again. I express my gratitude by saying a prayer. I honor and appreciate the water and Nature by doing so. It s become a ritual to me much like a baptism. Giving thanks.

I walk back up to the park bench. I zip up my parka and pull over my hood. I place my backpack over my shoulders. Time to go on one's way. I feel energized and ready to begin my walk back. I am now wholly present. Relaxed. Just waiting for something to come my way.

Spiritual Path

My meditative walk begins.

Cobb Brook is a truly remarkable landscape. It all comes together here at this vast open space. Where the mountains and forest seem to meet the river. A place where Nature truly puts you in your place - the present - all attention is here.

Having walked a few miles already, my familiarity this day and like many, is always made easy by the repeated landscape of this trail. Much like repeating a mantra over and over again. As I turn to head back, the terrain remains the same but my perspective has changed. I feel that I am connected to my surroundings. I'm just in it. I feel a part of something bigger. I feel safe.

I look up and see so much of the white sky, it appears bigger and closer than ever before. I'm surrounded by its snowflakes. Small fine snowflakes become bigger ones. Still falling softly but now a bit faster. I'm immersed in it.

A few more steps. I see trees to my left, trees to my right. The tree lines are more pronounced as they climb up their mountain sides. I'm surrounded by the forest. I'm just in it. Almost a black a white Polaroid picture.

I look to the river on my right, I can see so much of it, I can see how it bends 1/2 mile away. I feel like I am on top of it, a part of it. As I walk alongside it, I feel like I am flowing with it. Even the sound, the sound is not coming at you but with you.

A narrow path lies in front of me. Trees reach out to me from my left and from my right, partially covering the sky above me. The forest continues up the mountain side on my distant left. I can see so much of it. A few remaining leaves on the beech trees. The trees appear closer. A very simplistic view. Black and white. I feel like I am merging with it.

I keep walking. Silence.

At this point I realize that I'm just feeling better and better as the walk goes on. More feeling, less thinking. I only see my surroundings and feel my own body. I still feel the river hugging me to my right. Silence.

I am walking. No thoughts. Just walking. My mind is empty.

I look left. I look right. I see everything but not one particular thing. My attention has totally shifted to what lies in front of me - Nature and a part of me, a full part of me.

I am merging with Nature.

My feet now touch the ground. I cannot hear my foot steps. I feel the earth beneath me with every step- softer and more forgiving, almost as if I wearing slippers or moccasins.

My face and hands might feel a bit cold. I can only remember removing my hat and gloves from time to time. I feel my blood flowing throughout my body and the energy from the earth to my toes. Tingling feelings and an actual flow.

Calmness.

I feel my heart beat, steady and slow.

I feel energy moving through soles of feet. I sense mother earth's heart beat aligned with my own. I breath through my nose thru my head behind my eyes and feel fresh air moving down my spine into my chest. I sense a body change, a lightness.

I feel very close to my body and to this place I am in.

I feel my body in a new way, a stronger connection to my surroundings, a oneness. My awareness, my being, my energy is focused upon Nature's oneness, all relations.

All relations, meaning the earth, the water, and the air.

I hear nothing.

Quiet and stillness.

I have no thoughts. No worries. A clear mind.

how I developed a relationship with nature

Calmness.

My legs move steadily along with each and every step, effortlessly, no thought to my actions. Just in a flow.

I am now walking in sacred rhythm with the earth. Mother earth's heartbeat and my heartbeat as one.

I am clearly appreciative of the moment and the setting. Grounded and balanced. I am aware of my steps in the present.

Every step. Accepting my surroundings. Trusting it. Merging with them.

I am now approaching a significant bend in the river once again, my favorite place, the second vortex. Amazingly, and as if on cue, I spot a glimpse of a white flag bounding across my path, about 25 paces in front of me.

Moments later, I kneel down on my left knee by the stream and examine the tracks of a deer. I say to myself, sure enough a deer passed through here. The heart shaped hoofs are over two inches wide, maybe three inches long, and deep, perhaps those of a doe I am told later. The trotting pattern (about four feet apart) scamper off through a crevice in the mountain.

I did not realize it at the time but the deer's presence represented that a gentle lesson was about to come my way.

I stand, turn to my right, take a few steps, and kneel again. I cup my hands into my favorite stream and splash my forehead gently. I cleanse myself as I did only hours before while heading north on this very path, at this very stream. A ritual or baptism of sorts. I rise again. My feet planted in the earth, my palms extended to the sky, and my eyes closed. I pray. I give thanks for this moment, this place, and all relations. I honor and respect this place and all relations. Everything here and now is sacred.

I feel the tingling of energy between my hands. I can feel my blood flowing through out my body. I feel the energy flowing in Nature. My awareness, my being, my energy is focused upon Nature's oneness.

I am merging with Nature.
Something special is happening here.
Still very quiet, peaceful.

Peace Within

I have arrived. I have arrived at the second vortex. I open my eyes and notice that the canopy ahead expands outward and upward another 25 feet each way. My path follows the bend in the river. No more canopy. I see full sky. Snowflakes, snowflakes, everywhere snowflakes, to my left, to my right, straight ahead of me. Snowflakes. The ledges appear closer as they climb steeply to my left. The river appears closer as the shoreline disappears more to my right. The path climbs slightly and levels off at about twenty paces. Fewer trees appear upon river's edge. I feel a breeze. I'm a bit colder. Here, I feel exposed at this wide bend in the river with little land around me and high ledges behind me. I hear the oncoming rapids, louder than before, as they and the energy they bring, charge at me. I walk another twenty paces or so and stop on the far end of this plateau. Its suddenly very quiet. Yes, snowflakes. I'm standing still in my place, my feet planted in the earth. In the moment. Comforted in some way, blanketed in the snow by Nature. Part of a big picture as if playing a role in a slow motion movie or play. All attention is here. A oneness with Nature. I can no longer hear the river. I can no longer feel the breeze or cold. I can only see the landscape before me. All of my senses are locked in on my sight. A picturesque setting opens up before my eyes. I look over the snowy river, the snowy hills beyond, and the tall pine trees far against the snowy sky. Snowflakes calmly falling into place. Peace within.

I turn my head right to gaze at the oncoming river and I see. I see an older man. A Native American man. He is standing where I once walked by, only twenty paces away, by a tall beech tree, his side faces me as he stands by and looks over the river. I am startled

how I developed a relationship with nature

yet at ease. He is a strong man, my height and my build. Long gray flowing hair, below his shoulders. Plainly clothed to his wrist and ankles with soft, deer skinned leggings covered by a long, soft deer skinned shirt. No head dress, no decorated bead work, no colorful paint, no frills, no feathers. Perhaps, "in his younger days, of this man's duties, the most important was to acquire the skill and maintain the physique necessary to defend the tribe and to obtain the essential meat and skins for his household by hunting, trapping and fishing." (6)

My focus remains on the vision a bit longer before I turn my attention back to the river in front of me. I look beyond the smaller shoreline trees and once again notice the detailed outline of trees against the snow falling sky. They demand my attention. The majestic green hemlocks and pines appear taller and symmetrical behind the smaller mixed hardwoods that are front and center. They have a presence. I can count the snow covered branches. Snow flakes floating above us.

Seconds later, I looked right again, there he stands straight and proud, hands by his side, same as before, his weathered face, distinctive jaw and long nose, still intent on looking over the river. Perhaps, "in his mid years, he was a leader, a headman in a certain village who was respected for his quiet ways and good decisions. He did not ask to be a leader, but as a young man he had shown that he could think clearly and act calmly on the battlefield. And he was a good provider for his family and took care of the helpless ones. The people liked those ways and so they asked him to be a leader. This was, of course, in the old days. Today, in these times, men want to be leaders for the power and the glory of it, and not always because they have the good of the people truly in their hearts. So the man reluctantly became a leader, and over the years he made good decisions and always spoke the truth in the village council meetings, whether the truth hurt or helped. So for many, many years under his leadership the village prospered and was strong…"(7)

I return to looking straight across the river. The snow lays on the branches and the ground presenting a black and white picture. The wind swirls with snow to my left as the river passes by us. I glance over again, he still appears motionless. No feet. No foot wear. No feet to make foot prints. No foot prints. I had not walked by him. I could not see through him. He just appeared before me while all attention, his and mine were on the beauty of the river. We see the swirling wind and snow beyond us to the north, the distant mountains to our left and right.

Before leaving, all attention is on my vision of the elder. Although, he is looking out over the river, up towards the mountains and sky just as I, he knows much more than I. It is said that the most important responsibility of the elders was to share and teach the interconnectedness of all relations. "All Nature is a single in whole, formed, all of it by the creator and thus to a certain degree sacred. Trees are viewed almost like persons. Every man, bird, beast, flower, fruit or even rock has its role and special value as a part of the whole. Hence it deserves respect and if used by man, appreciation." (8)

One last look. Everything remains the same, and most of all, the white snow flakes falling quietly in between, in harmony and balance. No words were spoken just a shared appreciation for the moment.

All I can say to myself is wow, wow, wow as I walk further along on my path.

We are blessed to have elders amongst us.

I truly wanted to share my walk with someone this day. Looks like I did and will again with you. I continue to learn to this day what occurred in my first spiritual encounter. My relationship with Nature will be discussed in subsequent chapters.

Peace within.

Chapter 2

Developing A Relationship With Nature

When I was a child I played in Nature all of the time. I walked barefoot on the beach, playing in the waves, collecting shells and sand dollars ...I tried to catch leaves in the wind, jumped into piles of leaves, climbing trees... I tried catching snow flakes, sledding down hills, making snow angels...I danced in the rain, splashed in the puddles, swimming... Catching butterflies, fireflies, frogs, poly-wogs...Skimming rocks on a pond.. Smelling flowers.. Tasting wild berries.. Lay on the grass, looking up at the blue sky, at the many different clouds, admiring colors of a rainbow after a rain shower...Seeing things for the first time. It was always an adventure. I was lost in the moment.

As I went through adolescence, I spent more time in school and studies, sports, and relationships. Then on to college, more studies, partying and relationships. I graduated and moved from one job to another. As an adult I became distracted by modern day society and its technology- the responsibility of paying bills, watching television, reading newspapers, influenced by the aggressive advertising, the violence, focused upon relationship problems in my personal life and the work place. Fear based thoughts occupied my time. Who am I dating? What bills do I pay this week? Where am I going? Somewhere, I lost my childlike wonder.

In my early 30's I began spending more time outdoors. Recently divorced, two young children and more added responsibility than I ever imagined. I walked in nearby parks, hiked the Long Trail in Vermont, climbed mountains such as Mount Monadnock in New Hampshire, kayaked lakes and rivers in New England. Gradually, I began to reintegrate myself back into Nature and discover my own true nature. The beauty of silence and an opportunity to gather my thoughts. I began to grow. When alone, I acted as a child at times, dancing with the leaves as they floated in the wind, jumping from rock to rock in the streams and rivers, touching and smelling everything that crossed my path. And yes, I often stayed outdoors until dark. My relationship grew stronger and more comfortable wherever I was in Nature.

Short walks became longer walks.

New growth awaits us in Nature. Physically, mentally, emotionally, and spiritually, like any other relationship. Please read on.

Our Physically/Discovery Phase

A relationship will grow with time dictated by our lives circumstances and priorities.

So I walked and I walked and I walked...

I walked in all types of weather, all months of the year, and all days of the month and all hours of the day. Partial days, full days, weekends, and weeks, the longer the better.

We experience the elements in our daily lives from the morning sun rise to sunset. We experience the elements throughout the seasons from spring, summer, fall and winter. We are all connected through our life experiences. Appreciate all time and place in Nature.

Here are a five short stories to illustrate the uniqueness and sometimes, magical encounters we experience in different times of the day, in the different seasons.

Story #1

A Spring weekend camp out at Jamaica State Park. I anticipated a walk by day and camp by night. I arrived and walked five miles by mid afternoon. No concept of time. Warm in the shining sun, at times, shivers up and down my body. Very green. A strong musty smell of wet leaves. Nats hatching in the streams. Pink stars, buds and blossoms on the trees. A fast running river. Energy abounds. Its Spring. Song birds. A very balanced, relaxed walk despite seeing many people on the trail. Lately I had been paying attention to my feet. I feel very grounded with every step that I take is my own. At peace. Soaking my feet occasionally in river (at home with Epsom salt), here just in cold water. Nats and mosquitoes and myself at one. In fact, while setting up camp none bothered me, some flew about but not in the 20 minutes or so it took to put up a new tent and set up a camp fire on the river. An evening walk is more quiet. I sat quietly by a tree at river's edge, listening to the river and just before the sun sets right in front of me. Birds and chipmunks talking and saying good night to each other. Suddenly all is quiet, Nature sleeps again. A warm feeling comes over me, a love and appreciation for the moment or perhaps a love or appreciation by Nature. I return to camp and start my camp fire. I enjoy a cigar as I gaze into the fire. My mind drifts as I meditate unconsciously. Next, I read by candle light at the picnic table. I return to the fire and recite my prayers quietly. Later to fall asleep quickly, tucked away in my sleeping bag.

Story #2

A longer story still -spending summer time long weekends on the water whether in the Adirondacks in New York or the Connecticut Lakes in New Hampshire are great getaways to experience Nature from a different perspective -kayaking on the water. Although, we can find tranquil waters anytime we kayak, I have found these vast wilderness areas to offer more in diversity of the landscape and wildlife.

My story begins with a new day, kayaking on tranquil waters. A sunny day. A bright blue sky. A quiet day.

You gently push off from the sandy shallow waters where minnows abound. Just you and the outdoors.

I look around to see low growing shrubs and water plants lake side. Hemlock filling in behind them. Some standing, some lying down over the water. The winter weather and high winds can bend and topple over many poorly rooted trees.

The sun reflects upon the water, creating a "stars upon stars" affect on most of the water. Sparkling water everywhere.

You paddle effortlessly, pulling left and pushing right. Pulling right and pushing left. Continuing on, very quietly.

Quiet still. If you happen upon an exposed stream or river bank, you might see otters sliding down the mud and playing in the water.

With your upper body partially exposed and your bare legs, now balanced upon the top of the kayak. You enjoy the sun shining upon you. If early morning, we feel the morning mist.

Water bugs zigzag and land in the water beside you, creating small ripples that fan out to a large circle, much like when a child throws a stone in the water.

You feel the sun warm your face and shoulders down to your feet and toes. You are comforted in this yellow light.

Continuing on, peacefully.

how I developed a relationship with nature

You hear a warbling loon call from a distance.

You paddle effortlessly, pushing left and pulling right. Left and right again. Pulling left and pushing right. Silently.

Your eyes follow newly hatched dragon flies, their jewel like coloring, blue, green, and purple, darting everywhere, landing on your paddle.

Water drips so lightly off the end of a paddle.

Getting a bit warm, you cup your hands and splash cool water across your face and arms.

You pause and admire the blue sky overhead. Eagles are often perched amongst the highest trees. Always flying to different vantage points, always watching for meals below - unsuspecting ducks, especially younger ones (although I must say, the ducks are vigilant, their lives depend on it).

You approach the shallow waters in the marsh and see the rusty appearing water and smell the sulfur and methane gases from the decomposing plants and animals that have died here.

Moose are grazing on pond weed and grasses, sometimes as many as five.

You paddle effortlessly, pushing left and pulling right. Left and right again. Pulling left and pushing right. Very quietly.

You can be startled at any time by a beaver flapping its tail at you, telling you that you are trespassing on his waters.

Floating water lilies, yellow flowers above water, roots anchored below.

Drifting along to nowhere, so it seems. Stillness.

You spot a swimming loon in the distance. A portrait of beauty. Its black neck and white breast, its speckled black white body and its red eyes. She dives quickly underwater only to reappear again in the not too distant future. Sometimes, she will be carrying a young one on her back. And if you are lucky enough as I, you might see one loon lying amongst the reeds on a small island, nesting upon its eggs. (we should avoid disturbing any nesting loons).

Paddling on effortlessly. Pushing left, pulling right. Pushing left, pulling right. On and on. Silently.

Nearest right, a red winged black bird and later a blue jay follow you from tree to tree, branch to branch, peering at you. For you, a gift, an awareness.

At the back of the pond, painted turtles sun bath on logs, their shells and yellow and green necks and legs, drop into the water as you slide by them.

More moose grazing. And one time, just one time I was lucky enough to witness and a bull moose feeding in the middle of the pond. He would fully submerge to eat from the bottom and then rise his head and mighty rack out of the water, splashing and water dripping all around him. Below again and rising. What a display of stature and power. Below again and rising. Until he finally walks or swims ashore.

Floating along. Just you and the outdoors. You close your eyes. You see and hear nothing. A floating sensation comes over you. You and the water are at one with Nature.

Drifting closer to the shore, you awaken to a white tailed deer, waterside. Its narrow face and perked up ears looking straight at you. Gentle lessons are coming your way.

Paddling on effortlessly. Pulling left, pushing right. Pushing left, pulling right. On and on. Very quietly.

Now, full circle to the beginning of the pond. The loon appears beside you to share the love and light in this world and beyond.

Moving on, peacefully.

You glide into the landing. Small discreet waves roll in and spread out along the shoreline. Again and again. Roll in and spread out along the shoreline, so calmly.

Tranquil waters. Thank you for this day.

Story #3

A summertime weekend spent on the mountains, back to back days at the tallest mountains in the Northeast -Mount Katahdin at Baxter State Park, Maine and Tuckerman's Ravine in the White Mountains of New Hampshire will test your stamina and mind..

We arrive at Baxter State Park in the early afternoon and walk the many trails for miles and miles along the flat forest until almost sunset because that is what we do. Walk and walk, quietly and talking at times. We see green everywhere. Bright green moss on the ground, rocks and trees. Green plants, green ferns, and green hardwood and deciduous trees. Water everywhere, lakes, streams, beaver ponds, and marshes. Animals seen and heard everywhere, the deer, fox, moose, and ducks ….. The distant mountains. All is here in abundance and balance as it should be, the earth, the sun, the air and water. This is a lush, thriving, true wilderness.

We pitched a tent just before dark and awaken at sunrise to ascend Mount Katahdin (an elevation of 5267 feet) and named by The Penobscot Native Americans to mean "The Greatest Mountain." It took us a full day to climb the mountain just as advertised. Views of the valleys and nearby mountains to our right and rushing mountain streams and waterfalls to our left. The timberline, here, is higher than normal and always accompanied us on our left.

It's a long, steep, rocky trail. If there was ever a time when I would say as a child, are we there yet? It would be on this trail. My legs tired from the steep earth, my body hot from the sun, and sweat burning my eyes. We reached the near summit where we could sit down, let our body relax, and slow down. Be present. Enjoy the view of the blue sky and white clouds and the brown and green valleys and neighboring mountains. I can remember tasting the cold water and the chocolate power bar as they quenched my thirst and nourished my body. We could feel the breeze as well. A vastness and overwhelming experience for us.

We descended the mountain by sunset and rested that evening for another day.

Next day, meaning -climbing the second tallest mountain range in the northeast, Tuckerman's Ravine in the White Mountains. Tuckerman's Ravine is a glacial circle on the southeast face of Mount Washington (an elevation of 4186 feet). We got a late start on this climb. All I can remember are the large rocks and boulders we climbed over and the barren lands on this eight mile trail. More small shrubs and trees as you got higher on the trail. Only small game here, some rabbits, some squirrels, and birds. It reminded me of Mount Monadnock in Jaffrey, New Hampshire but more difficult terrain. My body fully exerted from days of climbing. Muscles working and breathing well. We stopped only for a few minutes below the summit, realizing we would be walking in the dark soon. I remember seeing rock and clouds. My body was tired and chilled as the evening cold temperature came upon us. The day hike turned into an evening walk. Carefully watching our steps in front of us. Being present in the darkness and silence. We finally arrive from where we began. My body begins to relax. Peace within.

Most everyone in New England are familiar with Early Fall walks. The colors speak for themselves. The cool air. Not too hot, not too cold. I sound like the Goldilocks. I've walked this path many times before and after the furlough day. In the rain, in the sunshine, in the snow, cold, daytime, morning and evening. Each time I expected to see the Indian spirit. Was I nervous? Yes. I have overcome that initial concern or nervousness of meeting him. Less apprehension. Evenings I' d walk out further on the path. I kept going back literally until I would step around and through a fallen tree on the path. Not knowing what is on the other side of the tree, I conquered my fear.

As the days get shorter -I walked all times of day, early mornings especially on weekends even during the week, usually afternoons, if out of work early, sometimes mid morning as this one 11 to 1 as I recognized it as the only time to connect with the outdoors because of work hours and darkness.

Story #4

I call it, "A two mile winter walk, not one". It all begins on New Years Eve Day, 2019. I am able to leave work by two o'clock this afternoon and walk out to my cabin. We have had three winter storms to date. The most recent two days, sleet, rain, sleet, and a few inches of snow. The storm had finally passed.

I park my car at the entrance to my hillside property. It's a winter wonderland. All trees and its branches are covered with ice and snow. Its an overwhelming white. No sunshine. A dull white sky. Bright white covered branches and ground. I had to wear my sunglasses to shield the white light. The picture was so clear. Black (brown) and white. Almost as if I were seeing it for the first time (but I had). It was that special. The air was cool and calm. I wore several layers of clothing - a long sleeve tee shirt, a work dress shirt, a hooded sweat shirt, and winter jacket. I brought a bottle of vitamin water and two head lamps and gloves in my pockets. The snow was packed down and solid to walk upon with my hiking boots and ice crampons and walking staff. I walked slowly and easily up the hills. I reach the forest and my steps sink one to two inches into the ground. Crunch. Crunch. I see some fox tracks that eventually join together and pair off in another direction. Further on, I see a set of rabbit prints hopping off into the safe cover of the brush. I smell the small vernal pool that remains unfrozen.

Lastly as I ascend to my cabin, I notice the small and tall hemlocks are weighted down by their ice covered branches. The white branches hang by their sides. They appear as small and tall inverted cones, human like cones. I have observed times where deer have made shelter in these smaller hemlock cone structures.

I arrive at the cabin and shovel the deck before entering.. Its 35 degrees inside and outside according to my thermometers. I walk about the cabin. I turn on the propane gas heater and sit nearby in my chair a while. I get up and complete my meditative postures and returned seated to meditate and pray....

The temperature is dropping, snowflakes are falling. Its time to leave the cabin. I turn off the heater and walk around the cabin before dressing again. I see the calendar on the kitchen wall and resist changing it to the New Year. Its December 31st but still not time to turn the page to another month. I have never been one to rush Father Time.

As I step down the deck, I hug both oak trees, left and right. These trees symbolize strength. These hugs are always solid ones. I feel like I'm hugging my father, receiving his love, understanding and support. I feel energized.

The distant mountain is blurred by the snow here and there, near and distant. My lips and nose are now cold.

As I meet the forest path, I hear my steps and staff upon the snow. My boots, crunch, crunch. My staff, ch ch ch (like a shovel digging into the soil).

Still snow white everywhere. Snow falling. No new tracks.

I descend my first hill and a crampon falls off. I reach down and notice the other one is missing, out of my sight. I back track almost all the way back to the cabin where I see my red plastic/steel crampon lying in the snow. I carry both in one hand and my staff in the other. When I descend the hills again, I walk heel to toe so as not to slip forward. Arriving at the car, a mile walk turns into a two mile one. All for the more fun.

Story #5

Lastly, I had to add this special winter walk encounter. I left an hour early one day from work to experience the few hours of remaining daylight that day. I wanted to clear my mind of human relationship thoughts and to meditate and pray in the present at my cabin. I wear a winter jacket, hiking boots with crampons, and my back pack filled with water, headlamps, gloves, and paper and pen.

Moving along with my walking staff in 35 degree or less temperatures, cloudy, still snow, still ice and bare covered ground. I climb my hills and face the forest and feel the presence of someone watching me, a strong feeling that it is the resident bob cat. I see no new tracks from here to the cabin. I look everywhere, especially places where I have seen her before -the ledges in the forest to my right, above and below, not to be seen. I look underneath the cabin deck and the ledges above the cabin, still no sign of the bobcat.

Once inside the cabin, I follow my normal routine -a walk about check of the interior, turning on the propane heater, meditative postures, sitting in silence, mediation and prayers. Some writing when I notice that it is getting dark, time to return to my car. I begin my ½ mile trek, looking again for the bobcat. The ledges, the brush, the ground/no tracks. I guess not to be this day. At my car, I remove my back pack, change my boots, and put my gear in the back of the car. Ready to go home. As I back up my car and look over to my left, I see some twenty feet away in trees, clear as day in the darkness, an illuminated figure, the bobcat standing and staring at me. Tawny fur, not red, not brown but in between. Standing sideways for only a few seconds like a camera flashed picture. Then dark again.

I return home to read about the bobcat once again in Ted Andrews book, Animal Speaks (9). The bobcat is a solitary animal that teaches us learning to be alone without being lonely. Hmmn.

The landscape and the elements of Nature

No two people perceive things the same way, especially the surroundings in Nature. I suggest to better enhance your experience, a walk where there is water, a diverse landscape, waterfalls, streams, rivers and mountains. A place where you can see different aspects of the elements in Nature.

All energy and life force come from the sun and the foods that we eat. The earths surface is 74% water and the rest is earth. We eat from the earth. Earth nourishes us and all living creatures. We all eventually return to the earth as well.

We belong here. Everything has its feet planted in the earth. We are grounded here. Always acknowledge the Earth. Always honor and respect every leaf and blade of grass. Be thankful as you walk upon it.

The water is everywhere, underground, and as water vapor in the clouds. Water is 64% of our body weight.

Air surrounds us. We are standing in it, all the way to our feet.

Wind and air breathes life into us. Focus upon and enjoy a breathe of fresh air.

"Our stories tell us where we come from and why we are here. In the beginning, these stories say, there was water, and then there was sky and fire, there was Earth, and there was life. We humans crawled out of the womb of the planet, or we were shaped out of clay and water, carved from twigs, compounded of seeds and ashes, or hatched from the cosmic egg. One way or another, we were made from the sacred elements that together compose the Earth. We are made from Earth, we breathe it in every breath we take, we drink it and eat it, and we share the same spark that animates the whole planet. Our stories tell us this, and so does our science." (10)

Recognize and appreciate the elements as you walk in Nature. To learn more about the elements including the night sky -moon and stars, and rainbows. Please review Chapter 5.

I prefer the level, clear path where I can look around rather than paying attention to my foot steps.

Learn about the landscape. Observe the landscape, the canopy, the ground, the water, the ledge, whirlpools, the sky, the mountain, the forest. The habitat determines what plants and animals you might see.

Find your place in Nature, a sacred place, a favorite place.

A comforting place that you are physically attracted to. A special place in Nature that makes you feel good. Relaxes you. Maybe a place where you are overwhelmed by the beauty in Nature.

Originally and always for me, it was the river walk. Then and always, the cave. Now and always, the cabin. My favorite place, my sacred place. To learn more about my sacred places, the walk, the cave, and my cabin, read on to Chapters 7, 8, and 9.

Find a quiet, secluded place off the main path or in the middle of the river. Two stories follow.

Story #1

An April Jamaica walk. I walked the entire path w/boots, stopping several times, at a water fall, streams, to the Cobb brook just enjoying, relaxing, meditating. There is much energy at the brook and a balanced consistent energy over the river. A strong stream of energy from the sunlight over the river comes through me. At one point, the mist from the water circles around me from the rushing river.

Story #2

An April day, same path. I walked a few miles and sat on a large boulder riverside, relaxed, and meditated. I see large clouds of energy rolling from the bend in the river towards me continuously, one after another. I feel energized. A vortex exists here. To learn more about a power of place and vortex, please read Chapter 6.

I now begin with the four stages of development with Nature.

1. Physically – Develop and Engage the Senses

Begin with the simple experiences in Nature - walk, sit down, lie down, feel the ground, feel the breeze, feel the sunlight. And lastly, someday see and feel the energy.

Sense of Sight

Pay attention. Look, listen and feel as if you are walking there for the first time. Look for any movement on the forest floor or the canopy above you.

Story #1 Sit and be quiet happens on 09/19/2001.

The recent fear based events of 911 are examples of distraction. I walked a well traveled path behind a Walmart Store. I intended to find a quiet place to meditate and pray. A blue jay flew across my path and led me to a lower, secluded trail with many surrounding old hemlocks (a confined area). I followed and sat there, my back against a pine tree with a strong intention of love and prayers. Three blue jays appear to me in the trees. 50'30'20'away and coming closer and watching me. Many chipmunks ten or more on each side of me 10' away. I can hear them moving, talking, and see them. Wind, nuts falling, leaves falling. The sun shines through this forested area. Sitting, I perform my Tai chi exercises and silently recite prayers. My chakras open. Be present.

Story #2 Sit and be quiet in the middle of a river.

I hop from rock to rock until I'm in the middle of the river. I sit down and relax and looked up and down the river. I remove my socks and boots and soak my feet. I lie down and meditate in the sun. I see butterflies, one in particular circling my head and lands beside me - brown, blue, black and white. Dancing about. Its message, a transformation will take place. The colors mean brown as grounded new growth; white as purity, sharing and truth; blue as happiness, calmness, truth, and black magic. (11)

If you sit still in Nature, you will see all there is to see.

We have the ability to increase our vision, perception and awareness.

Observe the edges, the ocean and shore with its waves; the forest and meadow. Look around, walk comfortably, walk slowly, observing, no hurry, its not a race.

In the Fall - look across the mountain and notice the detailed outline of trees, count the branches, see the barren ground. Are there any animals walking about the ground?

Look closer at the branches, the end of the branches, the buds. Some buds open earlier in the sunlight, nourished by the sun. Colors popping out at you - green, foliage red, orange, and yellow.

how I developed a relationship with nature

Story #3 Looking at animals.

Look up and around. One June day. I saw a deer in the Green Mountain Girls camp driveway. She stared at me awhile then pranced into the woods. I later walked the river path. I could feel the air around me, see the green and blue sky above me, and hear the running water, and feel the earth beneath me. I walk to where I saw the Native American spirit and upon that space, a green hawthorn leaf fell from above and I caught it at this very spot. This leaf symbolizes creativity, fertility and magic. No other leaves falling but this one. Its June, not October.

Look around. See the light, colors, shapes, and textures. The space. Listen to the sounds. Touch something. Feel the air. A high vibrational frequency in you and around you. Great stillness and peace. Complete acceptance of where you are and what is, no fear. The silent presence of each thing. Just being, plants, animals, the forest and river do it best.

Story #4 A winter time walk.

Keep looking and connecting with animals. I sense a change is coming my way. I hadn't been out in awhile due to snow/ice storms and other commitments the past two weeks. I smudged myself the evening before. I went snowshoeing at Jamaica State park from 1 to 515PM. I grounded myself with white light before I continued. Everything popped out at me, the green pines, the water, the brown tree trunks and branches, even the overcast misty day seem bright to me. One foot of snow was on the ground, crusty and frozen. I came across only one cross-country skier and person snowshoeing on the way in. I realized that I must set aside more time to focus and develop my connection with Nature. I am walking through the pines and hear a bird off to my right, keep looking but see nothing. This continues for a few minutes, still hearing but not seeing. I could now hear the rain drops panging against the hard snow ground, sounding like loud bells at times. At about halfway 1.5 miles, I tire and rest while facing the river. An incredible white light, so bright for an overcast day. I open my eyes and see a brown figure across the river, a large brown deer, very still, looking at me. It blends in well with its surroundings - a sandy, dark shoreline and snow in the background. Both of us still for 15 minutes. I sense a connection. I send my love and calming energy towards the deer and receive it in return. There is a strong connection over the river. I send kisses to the deer and it moves its ears. No antlers. I move on, looking back occasionally. Almost to the brook, my destination and I hear the bird again only this time its on my left side coming from the other side of the river. I look up and spot it - an eagle, brown not as large as ones I've seen in the past. Its speaking to me. It flies from one high pine tree perch about four times before flying down river. It was almost as if it wanted me to follow but I was determined to do what I always do here - I splashed my face with water and meditated for a short time. Halfway back, I met the same deer in the middle of the path. Maybe 50' away. Still and looking at each other. I expect the deer to move towards me but it suddenly darts into the wooded mountains as a couple comes around a bend in the path ahead of me. I watch the white tail climb the gulley and into the hills. It looks back as well. I made a friend and totem. Upon my return home, I read about what the deer symbolizes gentleness and innocence. A gentle luring adventure for next five years. They adapt well to any habitat. Can be a reminder to move back gently to the traditional family unit and roles. Deer senses are acute. Their vision and hearing especially. This totem will find increasing ability to detect subtle movements and appearances. You may begin to hear what is not said directly. A new innocence and freshness is about to be awakened. New doors to adventure for you. (12)

    I believe if you see animals once, your eyes become trained to see them again. To learn more about seeing animals, read on to Chapter 3.

    Observe the flow of energy in the sunlight, water, and wind. We experience energy in every day life when we see it, hear it and feel it.

A way to see energy is by possibly a soft focus on what lies in front of you, blur your vision.

To see and feel the energy became natural for me and can be natural for you as well. Don't be afraid, embrace it and grow with it.

To learn more, see Chapter 6 Recognizing Energy.

Sense of Touch

Walk slowly, feel your feet touching the earth, become aware of all life around you. Touch the water, touch the moss. Pay attention to your warm body and cold hands. Is your face cold? Touch your face.

Walking on pine needles. Walking on a hard path. Are your feet comfortable or tired and cold. Are they sinking in the snow, earth? A difficult walk, a leisurely walk?

One story to tell. An April springtime walk.

On the same path. There was a kayak race the day before. Therefore, the water was rushing out of the dam. A beautiful day. 64 degrees, sunny, breezy, a consistent energy. I walked almost to the end. I found a rock with layers around it. I had a desire to wash my feet. Rolled up pants, socks and sneakers off, I dangled my feet in the cold water. I splashed my face and hands as always. The running water, sun and breeze perform the cleansing. My hands feel the energy pulling from the earth below and the sky above. I feel a connection in between the two.

Sense of Hearing

My sense of hearing is very acute in Nature. Generally, when I return home I am very sensitive to the new surroundings/home again.

Listen consciously and listen deeper, hear the leaves in the wind. Listen carefully, listen for any movement on the forest floor or in the canopy above you.

I feel that once I heard the few remaining beech leaves in the fall and winter breeze, I began to hear everything. Including the animals in the nearby and distant brush.

Hear song birds.

Our hearing can be enhanced and developed throughout our lives.

Sense of Smell

Breathe in and out of your noses. Open your noses and smell the scent. Everything has scent. Smell the wet leaves on the ground, the standing pine, the air.

Take the time to breathe in the fresh air through your nose. Breathe in and feel your lungs expand. I had a tendency, more so in the Fall and Winter for my sinuses to open up and drip. Take the time to smell the roses as they say.

I can recall when I hiked to the cave many years ago. From the very onset of the trail, one mile away, I could smell the perfume of some of the women unbeknownst to me hiking the same path that day. Sure enough, when I arrived at the base of the mountain, they were resting, to climb to the summit.

We have the ability to increase our of sense of smell. I'm sure many outdoorsmen have a keen sense of smell they have developed over the years. Relate to the scent once and you will recognize it.

One example of engaging all senses: A March walk combining the Winter and Spring seasons. Where else, Jamaica State Park again. Forty degrees and sunny, not a cloud in the sky. Melting snow yet still an eighteen inch base on trails. I sense lots of energy today. Some earth uncovered. I can **feel** the impressions in the sand on the driveways and parking lots. I snowshoe on the river path. **I hear** the river running even the distinctive sounds in the slow flat spots. The ripples appear defined as well. I am tuned into the sight and sound of the river. Large rocks to my right still covered with snow. Wearing sun glasses to protect the brightness, I could still see the energy. A very high vibrating day as expected. No foliage above, the sun shines down on river. I feel the breeze, however, the wind only blows along the lower valley or river. The bottoms of trees and bushes moved, the tops did not. Winter yet spring in the air. I pause several times, sit by the river, look it over, look up the mountains to the sky. I see lots of energy and spirit I have never seen before - they appear to be yellow bodies (two lines like wings) moving up from water to the sides of the mountains to the sky. My eyes follow them. Spirits? Energy? Or both. It's a very intense energy above the water as I could see with my sun glasses on. I normally take my glasses off to see energy. Back to the river, no ice flowing, only ice on the sides. I could see the brown bottom of the river. Energy moving above the river, moving the lower tree branches . A very special day. Yellow bodies of energy, spiritual bodies. Different shapes, not human form, round shapes, some longer, some shorter. Many prayers said for many. At the end of day, a three hour walk. I opened up and took in the day and Nature in turn did the same for me. The message of the day- our state of mind is very important. We must do that.

Changes are constant in the outer world. While in Nature, stable and at peace.

Sights and sounds make us think. Touch and smell make us feel.

Listen to your thoughts. Be mindfully present and at peace while walking in Nature. The messages we receive are very important. They teach us. They strengthen our existing relationship with Nature.

Thoughts pop into my head - usually as I leave or after a meditation - messages come to me. Here are two such experiences.

Story #1

An April morning river walk. Snow melted until entering the woods, then ice. Stopped at large rock in river, but was to continue but wearing sneakers and ice slippery. Climbed down to river and laid on large rock facing up river. Blanket out, a strong spring breeze and bright sun. Said prayers. I heard the eagle again. I saw an outline of an eagle spirit come towards me and go up river about 20 yards away. In an area of fast moving water, I meditate more. I see two beautiful common terns fly up river, one past me, one past me moments later. I also have a vision of fire on end of a branch, and again the same vision. I sense it was time to leave. I am told to cooperate and teach others, be a leader and tell the truth. A branch of fire signifies "the above". Learn how to believe and work in other dimensions.

Story #2

Another message came on a July morning Jamaica river walk. Everything green and beautiful. Felt energized the moment I walked in, 6 oclock ish, the temperature cool, wearing a long sleeve. Immediately in tune with the earth. I felt energy pushing up through soles of my feet. Walking in a flowing motion. I felt energy pushing down and entering through the back of my shoulders - a tingling and numbing sensation. I stopped at big rocks, sat on one in the river, energy moving and swirling down and up, whirlpools, a lot of energy. Goose bumps. A message - we can start all over with Mother Earth, become environmentally active and a spiritual teacher.

2. The Mentally/Stability phase

This phase is simplest to explain but might take time to obtain.

A mind clearing walk. In society, we see many things going on, busy energy, many directions being taken, and a lot of anxiety.

When I first began walking it took time to get out of my mind. Lots of walks, short ones, long ones, almost daily, over years. As my relationship with Nature grew. What used to take me forever, became 15 to 20 minutes to come to peace, and now miraculously just a step into the woods and I am at peace. I am mindfully present.

how I developed a relationship with nature

We begin to notice more. We pay more attention to the small things. The small things are simple. Our mind focuses upon the landscape and what is around us, the simple things…..We move away from our thoughts and focus on the present.

We begin to ask questions again. A child's curiosity. Picking up things, touching everything, smelling it, maybe not tasting it but in some cases, eating wild berries.

We begin to recognize Nature as our stable partner. Nature only changes as the season changes. Nature is true to you. No lies, no spins, no stretches. Only the truth.

Our ego, our busy mind and fear based thoughts are left behind.

There is no judgment as to what is going on in Nature. What is, is. The sun rises, the sun sets. The wind blows. The streams and rivers flow. The circle of life, the earth, water and sun nourish the plants. The animals eat the plants……and so forth.

Most importantly, we learn how to live in the present moment. Avoiding distractions and stress. We can learn to meditate, focus on the breath, and focus on the rhythm of your heart and mother earth.

Remember to engage your senses. Our life will flow in Nature, then at home, and then in our community.

We have learned to remain calm as there is no fear such as rejection in this relationship. We can only grow in our relationship with Nature.

Your role as the student is learning by being yourself. There is no role playing with this partner, Nature. You only must be willing to learn. Nature can provide a grounding for us as well. There are many lessons to be learned.

We can learn many things in Nature from all living things and the meanings behind them. The animals, the elements, the energy and the favorite places we might visit. The chapters to follow teach us these things…

We are comfortable, we feel safe. With our acceptance, we move forward to the……

3. The Emotionally/Commitment phase

I had always appreciated the outdoors but now I was committed to it. I had feelings for Nature. I listened to Nature. I loved Nature. I cared for Nature.

We are spending more time together. I am almost outdoors on a daily basis. Especially weekends, walking and kayaking.

Eventually an attraction will exist between us. More time might be required and a pulling if you ignore it, especially if I had not been for a walk or the next few days appear certain that there would be no time for one. Best described as wanting to see your lover, a girlfriend or boyfriend. Three stories illustrate our emotional commitment.

Story #1

Back for a moment, to my initial vision experience. I had entered the park with the external influences beside me. As I left, I stepped out of Nature with a feeling of bliss. Nature had wrapped itself around me with snow. I hadn't yet figured out what happened with my vision. I had no thoughts, just feelings. More snow surrounding me, I was flowing out of the park along with the river. More snow surrounding me. Moving along faster, not floating, just flowing along. A feeling of love. Nature loved me as well.

Shortly thereafter if not before this experience, I recognized the significance that all relationships are related. We care for everything related, all relations. Everything is special and related. All relations are sacred. We can develop a relationship with an animal, plants, trees and places.

I began to recognize the importance of Nature as my primary relationship.

Story #2

A subsequent Jamaica river walk provides this very lesson. I walked a few miles to Cobb brook and lay hidden below the paths.

Both the river and brook face me. I said my Nature based prayer, very slowly, very deliberately, pausing in between my thoughts and prayers. At a glance out of a corner of my eye, one bird, then two birds fly nearby, about 25 ' away. Still meditating, it did not strike a significance at the time. Moments follow and far up in the air, 200 ' away, a male eagle appears. I say to myself, "just me and Nature". Moments follow that one and a female eagle comes into view, larger, riding the air currents. Two fly byes by each bird high in the sky. My interpretation, Nature will be my primary relationship, and perhaps one day, a woman will come into my life. There's always a lesson to be learned if we are open to it.

Story #3

Yet again, my last story. Appreciate the heart connection we might have with the earth. I have always been attracted to pine trees despite their sticky sap. Their bright lime green tips, their new growth. They often appear in stands of a couple feet high, 4' high, 6' high. On this path and others you might walk through a valley of these saplings. They pop out at you. From time to time, I stop and really focus upon them. This day, they covered a hill side below me. I grabbed a birch tree next to me and felt the warmth as I had with the smaller pines. As I turned away, I felt the pines sending love to me and my eyes welled up with tears. Tears of joy. The wind picked up and the tall birch was swaying high in the wind and gradually the smaller pines swayed as if to say hello and goodbye.

With our acceptance and commitment, trust what is there.

No truer place getting to know yourself, your own being no external influences. Leads us into next phase.

The Spiritually/Responsibility phase

We all hear stories of traumatic and near death experiences that can influence our spiritual lives.

It's a bit different here and Tom Brown describes it best, "There is no separation of nature and spirit. Nature becomes a door way to spirit and spirit becomes a door way to Nature. There is only the sacred oneness that we are all part of stepping in that door." (2)

When you are walking, you are walking your path. Your favorite place in Nature - a forest, mountain, lake or river becomes your power of place and sacred space.

How? "Place involves a relationship. As we explore, commit, and remain present over time, we bump into our limitations....as we commit ourselves to place, it unfolds its wonders." (13)

My spiritual world unfolded before me when I accepted the responsibility that came with it. I returned several times to Jamaica State Park after my first vision, mostly during evenings because of my responsibilities and the time of the year. I wanted more of what I had just experienced and wanted more peace and comfort surrounding those type of experiences. I finally walked as far the bend of the river. I symbolically passed through a downed pine tree in my path. I was willing and able, open and responsible to accept all spiritual encounters before me.

I knew that I had discovered something special and had the responsibility to share it some day with you. My relationship with Nature would grow quickly and I looked forward to the new beginnings and experiences. I learned about myself as I became physically, mentally, emotionally and spiritually connected and in tune with mother earth. Many lessons would follow and at times, flow.

Story time

One such experience happened on an October day. Where else? One of my favorite walks, Jamaica State Park. I walk along the river wearing two layers of clothes, long sleeve shirts. Still a chilly 30 degrees. I also wore my purple woven blanket around my shoulders, tied in a knot in front, never worn this way but today, it fit just right. The river appears to be of gold as the sun reflects upon its waters. Colors of yellow spot the river as well. I feel my foot steps on

how I developed a relationship with nature

the damp ground. Leaving prints, sinking in slightly. Many colors, still. Plenty of green. Some leaves falling. Some blankets of leaves on path - gold & yellow. Some red. I eventually gave my mother this blanket. It had been many places the past two years (the cave for one), heard many prayers, many rituals, had caught a green leaf that I gave her as well. I stopped by a deck area and wandered down a ways to a secluded area by the water. A red berry bush to my right and gold beech leaves behind me. Ground cover to the left. I sit on a large rock, my legs crossed. Recite my prayers. The rushing rapids carry away my un pure thoughts of the past four weeks. I gazed up at mountains from time to time. As I began walking again, I say to myself that will only catch a leaf in my blanket knot by my throat otherwise I am not catching one with my hands. I come upon the small brook where I always wash my hands and bless myself. As I reached over and cupped my hands with water, a gold leaf falls onto my knot. Thank you, I say. I walk upon beds of leaves. Sun streams of light come through the canopy above. I step in them unintentionally and intentionally, I always stop. There they are, coming through the trees, providing warmth and strength. I stop again at a slow moving river spot, another favorite spot. Look up and around, enjoy the views. Move on. I wander down out of view and stand in the light. Saying prayers, holding the light. This special day, I would later meet with my mom and share my spirituality and my great appreciation for Nature. I see three angels supporting her through her surgery. She later felt the presence of the angels in her condo and in the hospital hallway leading to the operation room.

    I had learned from the Native American elders that all relationships in Nature are related.

    I was thankful and honored the sacredness of the circle of life.

    I became one with Nature in my home and in Nature.

    I would recite more and more of Nature based prayers at my home and my home in Nature.

    My Nature prayer and you will likely hear it again:

We call in the East Wind. The direction of spirit (and its totem, the eagle). To bring greater power to our prayers and intentions. To provide us with clear vision and awareness, new beginnings and enlightenment. We thank you.

We call in the South Wind (and its totem the deer). The direction of growth and expansion. Give us the strength to expand and learn. Give us the strength to heal. Give us the strength to heal. Give us the strength to heal. We thank you. Thank you for live's gentle lessons.

We call in the West Wind (and its totem the mountain lion). Allow us to look within ourselves. To find harmony and balance. To find harmony and balance in all aspects of our lives. To find harmony and balance in our physical, mental, emotional, and spiritual lives. To find harmony and balance in our personal, family, community, church, love, work and play lives. We thank you.

We call in the North Wind (and its totem the bear). May your wisdom bring us insight. Show us how to understand our knowledge, how to use our knowledge, and the consequences of our knowledge. Show us how to be honest with ourselves. Show us how to be honest with others. Show us the truth. Show us the truth. Show us the truth. We thank you.

Grandfather Sun Thank you for your warmth and strength.

Grandmother moon Thank you for your changing faces and influences upon us. You make our lives so interesting.

Mother earth. We thank you for your many gifts. Please continue to provide us with your energies which will strengthen our connection to you and everything around you. We thank you.

We call on the Almighty Spirit, Sky Spirit, God and the elders and all those who honor and respect Mother Earth to join us in prayer to protect, preserve and replenish our natural resources. Our lands…., our waters….., our skies…., our sun, all habitat…., all species….We thank you.

Summarizing,

how I developed a relationship with nature

We learn more about ourselves as we become physically, mentally, emotionally and spiritually connected with Nature. We become in tune with mother earth. We can do this by performing simple activities in Nature. Smell the fresh cut grass on the ball field or golf course. Pick it up, sift it through your hands, take a deep breathe. Water and snow skiing. Snow shoeing and cross country skiing. Kayaking on a tranquil lake - gliding and silence. Camping.

Look and think as only a child would. Inquisitive nature of a child - why why but why again tell me about the stars, the waves, the wind, why some branches blow in the wind. We should always ask or we will never get the answer.

Our childlike wonder, playing in dirt, catching leaves.

Listening to ocean in a seashell. And our child's curiosity - picking up things, touching everything, smelling it tasting it, as if we are seeing it for the first time.

Once you have developed a relationship with Nature, no one can take it away from you. It is a part of you. Learn more, please read on to the next chapters.

We are all related and all things work together in Nature.

Peace within.

Chapter 3

Seeing Animals in Nature

Pay attention. Look, listen and feel as if you are walking there for the first time.

Naturally, look and look for movement. Always look up, look for movement in the trees, the branches, the leaves, birds are always watching you.

Listen carefully. If you can hear the beech leaves in the breeze, you can hear everything. Listen to any movement on the forest floor or in the canopy above. Hear the frog jumping in the pond.

Feel the hard or soft earth beneath you or the warm or cold air against your face as you walk.

Smell the fresh air or the dampness left behind by an evening rain.

Dakota children understand that we are of the soil and the soil of us, that we love the birds and beasts that grew with us on the soil. A bond exists between all things because they all drink the same water and breathe the same air. (14)

All life is sacred. All relationships are related. Interconnectedness of life. We are a part of it. The animals are generally immersed in their senses in Nature and we must find ourselves in the same way. When I am in the moment and all of my senses are engaged, I am rewarded by it, blessed by their presence.

We have a sixth sense, sometimes referred to as instincts or intuition, utilized by many animals to warn them of impending danger. William Long calls it "presence" in his book, How Animals Talk. But first we will talk about how he describes his "child like wonder" When I was a child I used to sit long hours in the woods alone, partly for love of the breathing solitude and partly for getting acquainted with wild birds or beasts, which showed no fear of me when they found me quiet….As a child this faculty was as natural as anything else in life; for in childhood we take the world as we find it in personal experience, and nothing is especially wonderful where all is wonder. Perfectly natural, the instinctive attitude of a child, as of an animal, is one of curiosity rather than fear or destruction. If left to his natural instincts, a child meets every living creature with a mixture of shyness or timidity and bright interest. William often found himself in the presence of animals, them watching him, he watching them, or both when he" was most in harmony with the environment and a sharer of its deep tranquility"….(15)

Childlike wonder, children can stare for hours without blinking.

What are they seeing? What are they thinking? What are they expecting to see?

You will expect to see the animals. What will I see today? I am open to it, excited about it. See them once, your eyes are trained to see them again.

The more you track it, observe it, and read about it. The more you learn about it, you will grow and get closer with it. You will see it appear before your eyes, sometimes a flash.

Learn their meaning and about them and you will develop a relationship with them. How do they live? Eating, nesting, mating habits? Where do they live? What types of tracks? What type of feces? What does this sighting mean? Learn more about the animal, why was it there? What message might it have brought you.

You will hear how I developed a relationship with eagles in our next chapter but here are some other great examples.

The bobcat

Many years ago I saw a bobcat lying on a covered ledge above my cabin. Later that same year, I likely saw the same bobcat lying underneath the deck of my cabin during the approaching cold of winter. This spot also provides shelter and overlooks the cliff and valley below. Obviously, the animal trusted my presence as I did with him. He spent much of the winter underneath my deck. I never interacted with him, I only saw him when I ascended to the cabin deck from his opposite end locale.

I had read little of him at the time but knew of their preference for the high vistas like the other cat, the mountain lion. I began to read more about him when I saw him again years later.

Just before a sunset, sitting cliff side he or she was likely watching me clear brush below before it decided to move on. Moving close to the ground, cat like, at the bottom of cliff edge. A light brownish color? No noticeable tail. Close to the rocks and some forest cover with fifty feet diagonal distance still between us. Minimal or no eye contact. He leaped out of site in a matter of seconds.

I decided to read more about him in one of my favorite resource books. According to "Animal Speak". The bobcat is solitary and a great night time hunter because of its keen eyesight, sensitive whiskers, and tufted ears. It makes its home in rocky ledges. The females often have a small territory, but males can be quite nomadic, overlapping the territories of five or six females. Mating is usually in late winter, and then the males and females go their separate ways. (16)

I believe this to be my resident bobcat. He lives here, I am the visitor. I am sure that he has always been watching me, near or at a distance. Both of us, comfortable with the shared living arrangement.

The mountain lion

I truly believe that when we see some animals in Nature, it is not coincidental. They let you see them. One such totem of mine is the mountain lion. Many years ago on an early fall morning I walked up into the mountains near my cabin. A few inches of snow covered an open grassy meadow bordering rocks and forest. Large soft paw prints at least twelve feet a part. And to top it off, catlike feces to the side, not as large as one expect, but large enough. I shared with very few. Although, I knew mountain lions traveled vast distances in a day, I wanted this animal to remain undisturbed if still in the area. I shared my discovery with a local elderly man who frequently walked this road below me. He was not surprised as he had seen a mountain lion only a few miles away, one early morning, in the 1960's. If you talk with enough Vermonters, you will hear of even more recent personal sightings of the mountain lion. As I wrote this story, I heard of one such sighting in the town of Guilford, Vermont.

I have read a few books about the mountain lion. The mountain lion is believed to no longer to reside this side of the Mississippi river and extinct from New England since the early 1900's. The mountain lion is tawny in color, its body length three to five feet and can weigh up to 200 pounds. Its 2.5 foot long tail provides its balance while traversing the mountain sides. Mostly a nocturnal and solitary animal except during its mating season. Its acute senses of vision, smell and hearing help with its evening hunting and travels. It can live up to twelve years in the wild. This skilled climber frequently dwells in the trees. It can run forty five miles an hour, running jumps of forty feet and standing leaps of fifteen feet. It snarls and growls and hisses like a cat. It will eat any animal it can catch but prefers deer, one or two per week. It will drag the carcass to a spot where it can cover it with brush and will return to feed when hungry. The mountain lion is fierce, graceful, respected and feared.

Years ago, I recognized the presence and importance of the mountain lion in my life when I honored the animal with a tattoo of an adult and young mountain lion placed upon my right bicep. It also represents my relationship with my son Kaden.

Birds, birds, birds, everywhere

I am fascinated by birds and can often see them in the trees near or far away. Speaking of sightings, birds have generally been the easiest for me to see and hear in Nature. They move above in a visible sky, they move from branch to branch, they land everywhere on the ground searching for food and water. They speak to us. They speak to other animals in the wilderness and warn them of our approaching presence. Loons warn their own of approaching watercraft.

While on the Long Trail, I have had birds almost land on my staff if not for approaching hikers.

Many times, I hear mergasers flying over a river, hearing their wings flap against the air and in the water.

I see birds perching on dead branches that I elected not to cut that very day at my cabin.

Birds landing and feeding near me as I sit, still amongst the tall pines, appreciating the surroundings near the West River edge.

One morning on way to work I noticed and heard a crow a top a pine tree, crowing, crowing, crowing. Looks at me, I say hi and it stops crowing after I acknowledged it. A crow sighting can mean a magical or mystical experience might be coming your way. As you read along the book, I have had my share of them.

On an April afternoon on the way to my cave, I saw a white headed owl in a hole of large half living oak tree. Every time for years, I would look up at the same tree and see him. They say they fly silently. Perhaps when after their prey. While hiking, I have heard them flying amongst the trees many times. A barred owl let us know of his territory on a few occasions by doing his fly by over our cabin deck. It is also known for its great vision and hearing. The owl is associated with the moon, great healing powers, feminine energy, wisdom, and astral projection. They have a secret knowledge to share with you.

I have seen a hawk upon entering the meadow and the forest. It too is known for its visionary power, guardianship, keenest eyes, strong energy, life force, creative energies, and astral projection. It shares the same landscape as the owl.

My most prolific/wonderful interactions occur with the chickadees at my cabin. Especially after I sit, meditate and pray in my cabin. I will pray for two leggeds, then the four leggeds, winged creatures and more and the protection of our and their habitat. I observe many birds flying around my cabin, the deck, trees and ground. I look out every window. They are looking at me, whistling at me. I step outside, they are flying closer to me. All this after Calling in the Directions and my Nature prayer as follows:

Almighty God and Creator and Spirit in the Sky and Mother Earth, and… We ask for you to preserve and protect and replenish our natural resources, our sky and air, our sun, our waters, and our earth. To protect our habitat for all living creatures, big and small, four leggeds, two leggeds, winged creatures, finned creatures, appendage free creatures, all living creatures. Protect the waters, lakes and ponds, mountain brooks and streams, rivers, oceans, and small vernal ponds. Protect the land, forests, grass lands, mountains and valleys, deserts and ice covered lands. …..

Another day, another Nature prayer. My eyes closed. First a shadow. Then a buzzing by my head. I look out a window to my left, a chickadee, the next window, a chickadee is moving around the cabin from window to window.

Another day, another Nature prayer. My cabin door is open and screen door is shut. A chickadee is moving slowly along the log pile, looking over at me all the while.

What does this all mean? The obvious, they appreciate my prayer. But what do chickadees mean to us? The Cherokee Indians believed that these birds awakened our understanding and higher truth. (17)

Caring is attention. One winter day hike to my cabin. It was forecast at 25 degrees below with a wind chill as well We had had several days of cold weather like this. I was crazy to be out here but I had dressed in layers, a face mask and goggles. There was wind. Frostbite was a strong possibility if you did not dress properly. There was about a foot of frozen snow on the ground. Ice covered some branches. A group of chickadees followed me from tree to tree as I walked away from my cabin through the forest to my car. They were hungry. They were cold. I normally do not interfere with Nature but I later returned again that afternoon to brave the cold with a bird feeder, some rope and bird seed. I carried my step ladder a few hundred feet on my snowshoes to a group of trees where the chickadees had last congregated before me. I cleared any nearby branches and undergrowth to protect the birds from predators. I changed out of my snowshoes briefly when I strung a rope between two hemlocks. I hung the feeder and spread seed on the ground below as well. I returned early the next morning before church and filled the feeder one more time. I was able to return my appreciation and thankfulness to the chickadees by my presence and feeding. A relationship was formed. Caring is attention.

A baby seal

I can remember coming across an abandoned baby seal on the waters edge of the beach. We had a moment to ourselves before more onlookers approached us. My intuition told me to leave this baby creature alone. There appeared to be no visible injuries. We kept looking into each others eyes. A look of innocence and a story to tell. Perhaps her mother had gone feeding in the deep and left her unattended and safe in these shallows. I felt a strong need to connect and support this little one in peril as more and more people gathered. But not here and not now.

I retreated about forty yards and climbed a life guard station.

I sat and focused on her being for fifteen to thirty minutes. There, I completed some of my Buddhist postures, sending love and peace. I felt a stream of energy between us coming to and from my upper forehead. I am told that some state wardens eventually disbanded the crowd and little one was left on its own. Peace within.

We can also pray for a deceased animal. Many times I have seen recent deer lying roadside and sense their spiritual presence. Not only do I ask for their peace but I ask that the remains return to the earth from whence they came. We appreciate and honor the circle of life.

Deer

I have had many living encounters with deer. As the one described earlier in my vision, Chapter 1. They represent gentle lessons coming our way. Of course, I look for them. Why not? Deer are beautiful creatures. …..Like I said before, once you know where to look, you will see them. They are often seen at the edge of forest and meadow before sunrise or sunset.

I find that deer generally make eye contact. They stand motionless, I stand motionless. They stare at me, I stare at them. Their ears to the air, I'm listening too. Now is the time to communicate, appreciate their features and love the animal. Love the animal. Why not? You love your cat. You love your dog. We love domesticated animals. Why not wild ones?

Its amazing to see these deer up close. They appear soft and gentle as If you could reach out and hug them. Many years ago,

how I developed a relationship with nature

unexpectedly in my back yard, they fed on grass and traveled across yards into a local forest. Another time while approaching my cabin I saw what seem to be the two largest, healthiest deer I had ever seen. Tall, broad, one male, and a large rack of antlers. One doe, same build. They stared at me long enough to introduce themselves. Hi, I'm Big Buck and this is my lover, Big Doe. They scampered off into the brush.

I will see deer repeatedly in the same locations as I venture to my favorite meditative spots in Nature, be it the cave, a river path, the cabin. They help me feel as though I have returned to the wilderness while traveling along my spiritual path in Nature.

I'll share one more deer experience from many years ago. I walked my favorite river path for maybe 1.5 miles. I tired for some reason and rested riverside, hidden from hikers. I sat, grounded, facing west across the river. I saw an incredible white light, so bright for an overcast day. I closed my eyes. I open my eyes. A brown figure appears across the river. I focus, its a large brown deer, very still, looking at me. It blends in well with its surroundings - a sandy, dark shoreline and snow in the background. Both of us still for 15 minutes. I sense a connection. I send my love and calming energy towards the deer. I feel it return. There is a strong connection over the river. I send kisses to the deer and it moves its ears. I move on further down my path, looking back occasionally. Almost to the brook, my destination and I hear a bird again, only this time its on my left side coming from the other side of the river. I look up and spot it. An eagle, brown not as large as ones I've seen in the past. Its speaking to me. It flies from one high pine tree perch about four times before flying down river. It was almost as if it wanted me to follow but I was determined to do what I always do here. I splash my face with water and meditated for a short time. I turn around and walk back and meet the same doe in the middle of the path. Maybe 50' away. We remain still and look at each other. I expect the deer to move towards me but it suddenly darts into the wooded mountains as a couple comes around a bend in the path ahead of me. I watch the white tail climb the gulley and into the hills. It looks back as well. I made a friend. And a new totem.

Upon my return home, I read about that the deer symbolizes gentleness and innocence. They adapt well to any habitat. Can be a reminder to move back gently to the traditional family unit and roles. Deer senses are acute. Their vision and hearing especially. This totem will find increasing ability to detect subtle movements and appearances. You may begin to hear what is not said directly. A new innocence and freshness is about to be awakened. New doors to adventure for you. A gentle luring adventure. (18)

Lastly, real or imagined ? My thought has always been, if I think I saw it, I did indeed see it. Like seeing a mouse out of the corner of your eye, moving along, under the radiator in your home, beside it or in front of you. Put the mouse trap out, you will catch more than one.

Bear

My great example begins with walking on the Long Trail. A few miles into the trail, carrying provisions to last me three days. A heavy back pack in tow and sweating much on this hot summer day. I notice a movement, far away and over my right shoulder. I am startled, who is hiding from me and who is following me? I continue walking, a little faster, stopping at times, gazing back. Finally, I am able to focus on this dark figure as it appears, disappears, behind the green underbrush. A bear, oh my. I was initially concerned but I fear animals less than I fear humans in this environment. I was walking in his woods on his mountain. Yes, I was wary on my travels that day. Especially that evening, I did not sleep well while alone in the leanto. Turning my flashlight on at every sudden noise. When my three day adventure was said and done. It was a beautiful sunny and light hike through green, green mountains. Long range vistas, beaver ponds, moose droppings…. And no company, only a bear following me and protecting me as I hiked along the Long Trail. And a new totem.

I credit seeing the bear to looking upon the landscape around me, making my eyes open to see more. I noticed the movement and slowly focused in from there. Zooming in can be a valuable technique to seeing more animals in Nature. My sixth sense may have played a role as well. William Long describes this sixth sense as "a sense of presence" which he bases on the "assumption that every life recognizes and attracts every other life by some occult force." (19). I will call this mystical force, energy and will discuss it further in Chapter 6, Recognizing Energy. I might reference another example from Mr. Long as well.

I have seen a bear walking along the rocks in the valley below my cabin at times. I have heard them hooting often at night. Bears represent wisdom and insight in my Nature prayer.

Remember just like the bear, animals are always watching us even in the dark like the full moon experience I describe in the Chapter 5, Recognizing the Elements.

Lets conclude by stating the obvious. We talk to our cats and dogs all of the time. We love, befriend, honor and respect our relationships with our pets. Why not other wild animals, bobcats, chickadees, eagles, and deer……..

Be open, communicate as you would with your pet. Send a smile or warming thought. Simply watch and appreciate their features and behavior. Honor and respect these creatures.

To say it one more time, Dakota children understand that we are of the soil and the soil of us, that we love the birds and beasts that grew with us on the soil. A bond exists between all things because they all drink the same water and breathe the same air. (14)

We should understand that all life is sacred. All relationships are related, interconnected. We are a part of it. Be grateful for their presence in our lives.

Peace within.

Chapter 4
Eagle Speaks to Me

Many, many years ago, I recognized the presence and significance of eagles in my life. I cannot exactly remember when but I can certainly recall a defining moment and the meaningful ones that followed. I will share one here.

"All of a sudden, I see a bald eagle out of the corner of my eye. She circles around a tall pine to my right and is descending rapidly towards to me. I can see the white head and the white neck. I focus upon the approaching yellow beak and the intense yellow eyes. Then, with her expansive brown wings, extending some seven feet across its brown breast above me, she ascends just as quickly towards the hills, silently and majestically, as if to say to me "remember my spoken words".

Surry Dam

This all begins on a hot summer day shortly before noon at the Surry Dam in Surry, New Hampshire. Unlike Jamaica State Park, I had only walked here a few times. This is an immense, powerful place. The earthen rock-filled dam stands 83 feet tall and 1800 feet long. The Ashuelot river flows through the 253 acre reservoir. While mountains and 1600 acres of managed wilderness border the lake. It is much bigger than I as I begin to walk across the dam.

Spectacular colors of blue and green surround me. I look down, blue water. I look up, blue sky. I look in front or behind me, green grass and green trees.

It's a very warm day, ninety degrees. A clear blue sky. And the sun is shining so brightly. I'm wearing my hiking boots, tan shorts and a lime-green tank top shirt, my sunglasses and a red bandana covering my head. I have brought a small pair of binoculars, a bottle of sun tan lotion, and a large bottle of water strapped over my shoulder. And I always carry my walking stick. I'm traveling light for me. Just the essentials. No back pack. No power bars.

All types of recreation are allowed here, including hunting and fishing. Normally, there are people about walking their dogs or fishing by the shoreline. This day, I would see no one.

I cross over the dam and enter the forest to my left. Initially, I travel through pines, walking on a soft bed of pine needles and decomposed oak leaves. Dirt and small stones at my feet at times. I can see the reservoir for most of my walk amongst the trees. (as far as one hundred feet away).

There are piles of drift wood, discarded pieces of concrete, and piles of gravel along the way.

how I developed a relationship with nature

My feelings change, first Nature's presence, then man's presence.

My path remains dry except for a few wet stream beds.

I look around and see a variety of hardwoods and hemlock trees. Many branches, twigs, and leaves cover the forest floor. Many ferns as well.

The path appears well maintained and more Nature like either groomed that way by man or Nature's way of doing things.

I am mostly shaded from the sun except for a few spots where the sunlight peaks through the hardwood canopy. It is cool here.

I see less and less water as I go deeper into forest.

Ten minutes later, my path gradually ascends around to the right and opens up to the presence of enormous power lines. The towers stand tall and firm, six in all along this hilly path, supported by their iron and steel braces. They run parallel to the forest and reservoir on the left and to the mountains on the right. Maybe a one hundred foot open space in between. This is a fascinating place, tucked away where technology meets Nature, surrounded by its forest, water and mountains. All of Nature's elements are present. The earth, the water, the sun, and the sky.

I feel the ground beneath my feet whether its sandy, rocky or fallen grasses. The reservoir is about one hundred feet to my left and the hills a few hundred feet to my right. In between, shoulder height ground cover. Small maples, tall grasses, prickly berry bushes, and wild flowers of all kinds -, daisies, butter cups, black-eyed susans, purple flowers and weeds. Poison ivy at times.

I see many orange and black butterflies chasing each other. Bees and flies everywhere but not bothersome.

I can hear many small birds singing, chickadees and sparrows. And some larger ones, the blue jays. The chickadees remain hidden in the trees until one flies near the edge, then the other two, three or four birds will then follow to the more open spaces.

As I ascend the trail, I feel the sun beating down on me as if I am getting closer to the sun. Its hot, I can literally smell the heat.

Green trees are everywhere, standing to my left and climbing the mountains on my right.

I see small snakes slithering away before my feet at times.

It's not a difficult walk considering the number of times I am led up and down the hard, unforgiving trail, gradually climbing as I go. My focus on the surroundings makes my steps easier as I enjoy the adventure/this encounter. An occasional cool breeze from the direction of forest and reservoir helps too.

My path appears less traveled the further I progress.

This walk seems to be about more about looking into the wide open space, meaning the sky. I walk. I look up. I walk. I look up.

I am drawn to the sky.

Large rocks often appear on the side of the path, perhaps pushed aside when the power lines were being constructed.

It's a beautiful, calm day when…

I notice the wind suddenly coming down the valley, in my direction.

The tops of the trees are swaying.

I see and hear the leaves moving.

I feel the breeze.

Suddenly silence.

I look to my right and notice a large bird flying in the distance well above the mountains and the trees, a few hundred yards away. It's riding the high winds, appearing, and disappearing. Quick, I get out my binoculars. And I try to follow it but I lose it. I just know that it's an eagle because it's appears far, far away, soaring and reaching up into the sky, at times. It has to be an eagle.

I walk a bit further to a higher vantage point and lean against two rocks waist high there. I see more of the tree line, the mountains, and the skyline.

Tall trees and mountains surround me. I am at the base of the mountain and feel more of a part of it.

I feel closer to the sky as there is so much of it as there is the mountains below it. The mountains appear in the forefront and the sky in the background, framed in perfectly.

I focus in better on the skyline. I can see further now so it seems. This time, I spot the bird with my binoculars. it's a large bald eagle, likely a female.

A magnificent bird.

I relax and sit awhile longer. Its not just one eagle but its two! First a female, then a smaller male, both white and yellow. One disappears, the other returns. At times, I can see both gliding with the air currents across this sky. I watch for maybe five minutes.

What a performance in the sky. They're showing off their flying skills almost as if they are courting each other. Flying high and parting ways below.

I stand with my arms extended out and my palms up. Facing the skies, I express my thanks. I feel blessed by their presence.

Yi A Yer. Yi A Yer. Yi A Yer.

They're talking.

Yi A Yer. Yi A Yer.

The eagles are talking.

Yi A Yer. Yi A Yer. Yi A Yer.

They're saying the same message over and over again, in a high pitch tone.

Yi A Yer. Yi A Yer.

Eventually, I ask myself, what are they saying?

Yi A Yer. Yi A Yer.

I say to myself, I say to them. What are you saying?

Yi A Yer. Yi A Yer. Yi A Yer.

Yi A Yer. Yi A Yer.

I say live and learn?

Yi A Yer. Yi A Yer.

I say live and learn?

Yi A Yer. Yi A Yer.

I say live and learn?

Yi A Yer. Yi A Yer.
Finally an answer to comes to me,
No, love and learn.
Love and learn.
Love and learn. Love and learn I repeat to myself.
I am overwhelmed and almost brought to tears.
Love and learn.
Wow. What a message.
Silence.

A message delivered by the eagles. A message brought down from the heavens?

The eagles soon disappeared as I managed to walk back to the dam. My shoulders, face and arms were hot from the sun, despite the tanning lotion, I appeared red skinned. I was a bit shaken from the experience as well. I focused more on my steps forward than I had before and eventually made my way through the hills and forest. As I was leaving to walk across the dam:

"All of a sudden, I see a bald eagle out of the corner of my eye. She circles around a tall pine to my right and is descending rapidly towards to me. I can see the white head and the white neck. I focus upon the approaching yellow beak and the intense yellow eyes. Then, with her expansive brown wings, extending some seven feet across its brown breast above me, she ascends just as quickly towards the hills, silently and majestically, as if to say to me "remember my spoken words".

A few months later, the local Keene Sentinel newspaper reported that there was a nesting pair of bald eagles near Surry Dam. I would also learn that eagles are normally not as vocal as that day save for their courtship for one another. I believe that I indeed witnessed a part of their aerial mating ritual.

This day forward, I recognized the importance of and accepted the presence of Nature in my life. I was fully committed to our spiritual growth and the responsibility that comes with any relationship.

This encounter also prompted me to note my experiences with the intention of some day writing this book.

Eagles and their Spiritual Meaning

I have always been impressed by the readings of Ted Andrews in his book, Animal Speak. He offers his insight in the following descriptions below:

"The eagle is one of the greatest and most admired birds of prey. It has served as an inspiration to many societies. The fact that they are good at feeding themselves from the land and still soar to great heights in the sky reflects much about the hidden significance of the eagle who comes as a totem. They will teach a balance of being of the earth but not in it."(20).

To the Pueblo Indians the eagle was a bird of the sky with the ability to spiral upward until it passed through the hole in the sky to the home of the sun. It was associated with all the energies of the sun -physical and spiritual. From these heights it could survey all four directions, the north, south, east and west. They became symbols of greater sight and perception.

The white feathers of the bald eagles especially are often treasured as they are links to Grandmother Medicine - tremendous wisdom, healing, and creation. The feathers of eagles are sacred to the Native Americans, and since the eagle is protected by the United States government, it is a felony for anyone to possess such who is not of Native American blood (I am not Native American and possess no eagle feathers). The feathers, though, are used in powerful healing ceremonies (cleansing the aura) and even for shape shifting.

Both the bald eagle and golden eagle have come to symbolize heroic nobility and divine spirit. These eagles are the messengers from heaven and are the embodiment of the spirit of the sun."

Other noteworthy characteristics and their associated meanings are the vision and hearing of the eagle. The eagles have 3D or binocular vision, just like humans but they can see eight times greater than humans. For those with eagle totems, new vision will open, reaching into the past, present and future. Eagles also hear very well. Your ability to hear both spiritually and physically, will also increase.

To accept the eagle as your totem is to accept a powerful new dimension to life, and a heightened responsibility for your spiritual growth.

J.T. Garrett and Michael Garrett, members of the Eastern Band of Cherokee from North Carolina also share their meaning of the eagle in the following passage "When eagles speak you join the Circle with an open mind and an open heart, and to move at our own pace with clarity, kindness, and a sense of calm. To walk in beauty is to understand and practice the way of right relationship and to appreciate all of the beauty that exists both within and all around us…..he speaks in the way that he moves. He speaks with his eyes, with his balance, with his presence. …He speaks from the truth that soars in his heart and in his spirit. "(21).

I will always try to do the right thing. Love and learn.

A Relationship with Eagles

I decided to accept the eagle as my totem and our relationship grew rapidly from there. They became a part of all aspects of my life - physically, emotionally, mentally, and spiritually.

Physically -

My home was decorated with eagle pictures throughout my bedroom and living room. 10 X 12 wood framed pictures.

My mantle over the fireplace had two wooden carved sculptures sitting upon it.

Years later, I had an eagle tatoo engraved on my left bicep to recognize its importance in my life and share my appreciation for its presence in my life, on my own body.

Emotionally –

I began devoting more time to the eagles by visiting a local raptor center about one hour away in Woodstock, Vermont. My first visit began with acknowledging each bird.- the ravens, hawks, vultures, falcons, merlins, kestrels, and eagles. They were all visible facing me as I walked in front of and peered in each of their outdoor cages. First, I focused upon the golden eagles, a male and female, as they perched on a branches facing me together. A majestic bird. I could feel my forehead and eyes reaching out to them and connecting in some way. I moved onto the bald eagles because visitors were coming in behind me. This day, the bald eagles sat together as well. Again, I felt a connection, however, not as strong as the golden eagles. I stood there awhile and I visualized them flying free before and now perched in a cage. My eyes began to tear. I returned back to the golden eagles and I really connected again, I could feel the energy streaming from them to my head and shoulders. I found myself leaning in towards cage as if I was being pulled. I could feel the energy running up and down my entire body from my head to my toes and out again through my head. The male eagle eventually turned away. The female, not. I felt an overwhelming sense of love, a merging of sorts with both the golden and bald eagles. I often felt an immediate connection when an eagle came to the edge of the cage. I experienced some dizziness as well. I asked if they had any wisdom to share. Sometimes answers, often not. I sensed that the front part of my head broke away from me while standing before the golden eagles. Upon leaving premises at the gate, I felt a wave of energy coming into my shoulders & head, receiving it.

On another visit to the raptor center. I remember a time when the male bald eagle was talking to me. I recognized his high pitch voice and cry. I felt a connection again, though he eventually turned away. He did provide an answer, see below. The female eagle came to the edge of the cage for about thirty minutes. Head to head. Just sitting, looking, and listening. I sensed the energy just as I had before. The energy streaming from our heads through my body and out again through the top of my head. I became dizzy as well. This became a common theme whether I was drifting off in a kayak or walking a path when I encountered an eagle, I would feel light headed at times.

I believed that the energy pouring out of head and my light headedness was my crown chakra opening up. Something being shared between myself and the eagle, a euphoric feeling of acceptance/trust, love and understanding. On subsequent visits, I would often feel my same chakra open before I even arrived at the raptor center, to a lesser degree.

"Always try to do the right thing from my heart."

Mentally -

I began to study the eagles more and more by reading books and watching videos about them. I was fascinated so much that I began photographing them as well in Nature. By doing so, I understood the significance of their presence in my life. I appreciated every sighting. I honored and respected their presence. Mindfully, always try to do the right thing.

Spiritually -

I embraced the values they represent by referencing them in a portion of my daily prayer as it reads :"We call in the East Wind. The direction of spirit and its totem, the eagle. To bring greater power to our prayers and intentions. To provide us with clear vision and awareness, new beginnings and enlightenment. We thank you."

I incorporated an eagle mantra into my vocabulary which I cannot share with you. The mantra serves two purposes. One, it is my spiritual name for the eagle. And two, it is honored and respected in my meditation and prayers with the eagles and Nature.

To this day, they reach out to me and I to them as we began seeing more of each other in our travels. I see eagles often when driving

how I developed a relationship with nature

along country roads and major highways, or walking and kayaking various rivers and lakes. All the while, I recognize the outline and color of their feathers, their yellow beaks, and white neck and head. All in detail, as if I were focusing in with a pair of binoculars which I am not.

As I established a relationship with eagles I was able to see them more close and clearly. One Spring day I received a speeding ticket of $125 for traveling 35 in a 25 mile zone. The officer says 43 miles per hour. 3 points against your license. I don't even want to go to court. I felt penalized for being myself. Lots of thoughts - politics, society norms, statistics, establishment, town monies, authority. I was certainly growing more comfortable in the spiritual world than this one. I wanted to learn more and ready and ready to retreat from society. While driving through the Vermont country side later that afternoon, I saw the clearest vision of an eagle in years, flying maybe 50' above a field. My side glimpse presented a view of a yellow beak, white head, large brown feathers, beautiful majestic bird against a cloudy sky. This all outside of an old town, one general store and post office, farms with tractors left in the fields. I didn't want to leave this little old town.

The eagles represent my spiritual connection to Nature. This would all lead to a very sacred moment one evening leading up to my 40th birthday as discussed in Chapter 11 The Call from Spirits.

Peace within.

Chapter 5

Recognizing the elements

Our stories tell us where we come from and why we are here. In the beginning, these stories say, there was water, and then there was sky and fire, there was Earth, and there was life. We humans crawled out of the womb of the planet, or we were shaped out of clay and water, carved from twigs, compounded of seeds and ashes, or hatched from the cosmic egg. One way or another, we were made from the sacred elements that together compose the Earth. We are made from Earth, we breathe it in every breath we take, we drink it and eat it, and we share the same spark that animates the whole planet. Our stories tell us this, and so does our science. (22)

We experience the elements in our daily lives from the morning sun rise to sunset. We experience the elements throughout the seasons from spring, summer, fall and winter. We are all connected through our life experiences. Appreciate all place and time in Nature.

Nature sustains us. Everything plays a true role. We depend on Nature's actions, its life giving rains and sunshine. All actions and all seasons are deliberate. Nothing can live without it.

As spoken in Chapter 1 and here again, the interconnectedness of all relations. "All Nature is a single in whole, formed, all of it by the creator and thus to a certain degree sacred. Trees are viewed almost like persons. Every man, bird, beast, flower, fruit or even rock has its role and special value as a part of the whole. Hence it deserves respect and if used by man, appreciation." (8)

The Earth

All energy and life force come from the sun and the foods that we eat, The earths surface is 74% water and the rest is earth. We eat from the earth. Earth nourishes us and all living creatures. We all eventually return to the earth as well.

Soil affects the air around us by giving out and absorbing gases such as carbon dioxide, water vapor and methane.

Soil soaks up, holds, changes, and purifies most of the water found on land.

Soil acts as a home for many animals, fungi and bacteria.

Soil provides nutrients that plants and trees need to grow.

Soil acts as a filter to cleanse water before it seeps into rocks

Soil recycles nutrients such as carbon, so that it can be used all over again.

We experience the earth's energy when we walk upon the ground, the natural rhythm of the earth. Grounding ourselves. Its often been

how I developed a relationship with nature

suggested to walk barefoot. I enjoy walking barefoot on the beach. Walking barefoot or wearing moccasins in Nature might very well speed up the grounding process but for me the one time I hiked in moccasins for a few hours, all I remember was sore feet. Initially, I preferred sneakers if the terrain was not rough. Eventually, in a matter of moments, I became accustomed to the ground beneath me, wearing hiking boots or any footwear.

The earth's rotation contributes to the cycles of day and night, the weather, the tides, the fluctuations in the electromagnetic fields, the gravitational pull, and the light and sound waves cause a variation in rhythm.

We belong here. Everything has its feet planted in the earth. We are grounded here. Always acknowledge the Earth. Always honor and respect every leaf and blade of grass. Be thankful as you walk upon it.

Earth is wisdom. It is grounding. It is completing. It is the powerful inner knowing that comes from being connected to Nature, to the earth. It allows you to stand your ground in times of adversity. It is your health and the food that you eat. In Nature, Earth is the ground that you see, as well as the rocks and the deeply embedded stones and boulders, some of which you cannot see. Earth encompasses all those things that have their roots firmly within it, such as trees and plants. Earth is fertility and abundance and stability. Earth is physical power.

My prayer addresses the direction of the north as shows knowledge and wisdom and insight, how to use it and the consequences that come of it. We also ask Mother Earth to please continue to provide us with your energies so we might strengthen our connection with you and all things around you.

The Sun

The warm sun feels good and makes us happy.

The sun basking down, you're in it, lying on the beach or standing as I do. A ball of fire. Burn if you get too close. Look directly into it and it can blind you. Even as you are walking or driving along with sunglasses. Let me caution you how you use it.

Watch how the plants and trees reach up to the sun light. Straight up or bending around other competing growth.

Sunlight and photosynthesis grows green life. Three stories to tell about the sun.

Story #1

One summer day as I walk a few miles with a friend. I stop along the waters edge. The sunshine beams through my eyes down my body. Its warmth energizes me. I breathe in and out the air into my lungs, through my chest and entire body, invigorating. My muscles and body feel strong, yet relaxed. I am blessed in this moment. I hear all sounds near, windy branches, a crow, crackling trees. Suddenly, I hear nothing. I just see and feel the sun. Generally, I feel sexually energized or rejuvenated, if not that day, the next day, a strong feeling in my abdomen and lower back and pelvis region.

Story #2

On a winter late Sunday morning, 15 degrees, bright sunshine, a blue sky, and wind chill at my cabin, not a cloud in the sky. 6 inches of new snow covers a previously frozen foot of snow. I'm dressed in layers and a face mask. Goggles block the bitter cold and glare of the sun from my eyes. Not much sound, not even a crunch from my snow shoes. I can only and always will hear the beech tree leaves. The snow blankets the country side evenly, sculpted evenly amongst mostly bare trees and saplings. It looks like a white beach. Nature's wind treated the snow like the waves of the ocean treats the sand. I could see the ripples in the snow. The crystal snow sparkled in the sunshine like the water does in direct sunlight. There were some designs in the snow but again most notably, the curves and ripples you would see where the ocean tide moves back and forth on a sandy beach. I have always noticed the snow covered trees and branches and rocks but this day, it was earth covered snow. I could not hear the streams, for they are frozen. I notice tracks in the forest snow, actually near and by the cabin - mouse, fox and deer. Once again in the meadow, I tune in to the snow white covered ground below and the yellow sun in the sky above. I meditate, seeing and feeling its rays of sunshine as its energy runs from my head to my toes, throughout each chakra, energizing and aligning each chakra (chakras are discussed in the next chapter). My body feels great. The sun, its light and warmth invigorates me. I am excited. I feel mentally and physically strong. My lower body feels my sexual energy as if saying, this is where your back and pelvis lay. I feel energy throughout my entire body. I am thankful.

Story #3

On many walks like this Spring day walk along a Connecticut river path, I stop where the sun shines through a canopy and bask in the sun, looking up at it, recognizing it, praying and asking for a connection, asking for its warmth and energy. The sun shines through my top/crown chakra. I feel my chakra shift from my ankles moving up through my body, primarily as my head is being pulled forward towards the sun. I stayed in that position for awhile, I had trouble breaking away. What just happened. I had never felt such a strong connection before. I walk further along to a waterfall. I wash my hands and sprinkle my forehead with water as always. As I am about to leave, I see rainbow colors in the waterfall waters off to the right, then more, different bright colors. The water, the sun, and the air put on a show - a perfect interaction of the elements. I kept turning and looking. I could not walk away. I am thankful. I pray.

The sun provides energy to all living things on this earth including us. It sustains us.

What does the sun mean to you? How do you identify with it?

Again, my prayer, Grandfather Sun Thank you for your warmth and strength.

The Water

Water is everywhere, underground and as water vapor in the clouds.

The earths surface is 71 % oceans, another 3% lakes and rivers. Water is 64% of our body weight, babies 75%. The oceans stabilize the temperature of the earth. Whereas temperatures of the air change rapidly, the oceans absorb that energy and release it slowly.

Water quenches our thirst, 80% of our body, cleans our body, water to plants. Water we drink.

Baptizing my forehead with running stream water, washing my hands, submerging myself in a waterfall pool.

Pay attention to the distinctive ripples in the water and its waves on the lake or at an ocean

A rushing river, the energy within it, the energy above it, and the energy produced by it. Look for it.

The ocean and it's waves, bringing energy in with the tides, energy back out with its tides. The infinity of the horizon over the distance of the ocean. Magnificent. Immense.

Water is the most often recited example of a vortex. Water draining down a hole, spiraling down.

"The medicine power of the South is Water. Water represents feelings and emotions. It is our intuition. It is our deep connection to spirituality. It is your sacred dreams, psychic impressions and your inner knowing. It is the female part of your being. Waterfalls, the great fierce ocean, gentle seas, mountain streams, soft spring rains, torrential rains, the fog and mists, snow and ice are all Water in Nature. Water is fluid and soothing. Water is healing. Water is the power of emotion." (23)

My prayer references the direction of the South as healing and growth……

The Sky and Air

Wind and air breathes life into us. A breath of fresh air.
By definition, air is made of 78% nitrogen and 21% oxygen.
Air surrounds us. We are standing in it, all the way to our feet.
The weather patterns, low and high pressure systems, we experience these inversions. Pulling and pushing of air, cooling of air. Pushes ideas up and down from the cave of the earth. Wind and air, the warm air rises, then it cools and sinks forming a flow of air.

"The power of the East is the power of air. Air is lofty ideals. When a baby is born it takes its first breath of air. Air is new beginnings. It is allowing your spirit to soar. Light breezes, cyclones, dust devils, jet streams, tornadoes, whirling winds, warm winds and cold winds are part of the element of air in Nature. In Nature, Air circulates high above the land and has an overview of life. The part of you that is Air has the ability to see afar. It is that part of you that is universal. It is illumination and integration, freedom and movement. Air uplifts, exhilarates and expands. Air is your thoughts. Air is power of the mind." (23) I believe it to mean our strength in our prayers and intentions. New beginnings, clear vision, awareness, and enlightenment.

Lastly and always, a cool breeze soothes us, and sometimes just enough to let you know the air is there against our face.

The Moon and the Stars

As children, we were fascinated by the night sky, the moon and the stars. It all started with the children stories and myths told to us. The man in the moon. And lest we forget the rhyme, Mr. Moon, Mr. Moon, you're out too soon, go back to bed and rest your sleepy head…..

The Moon

Man in the moon face, only one face. The moon orbits the earth in the same amount of time as the earth spins on its axis. We never see the other side of the moon because the gravity of the earth slows the rotation of the moon to the same rate as earth.

The cheese.

I have taken many full moon walks, some alone, some together. Regardless, always no fear. The moon normally lights up the forest and the path in front of us.

One, such special full moon walk with my pre- teen daughter at Jamaica State park stands out. It was a cloudy, cool evening in November. We had used flash lights on our two mile walk (always carried spare head lamps) to one of my favorite sitting spots on the river. All alone. As you get deeper and deeper into the path or woods you can see pairs of animal eyes across the river, especially where Cobb brook meets West river and the mountain really rises. I remember looking over the river wishing that I could see it all but could not because of the darkness and cloudy sky. All of sudden the entire river lights up in front of me. I thought a car had quietly pulled up behind us and flashed on its high beams. I turned around and noticed that the full moon had appeared from behind the clouds and mountain. This spectacular sight lasted awhile. The waters shined in the moon light. As the moon disappeared behind the clouds, we walked away.

The Dancing Stars

Favorite children's stories, twinkle twinkle little star and wish upon a shooting star. Stars do twinkle and sparkle of course, in short physics, cells and bending light.

Yes, shooting stars are real too. Appearing as brilliant meteors.

Star constellations, the big dipper, the little dipper, little bear, great bear, lion….and the bright north star.

So many in the sky.
Seem much closer at times.
Dipper, little dipper.
Just on top or behind the trees.
Different location every time you look.
Learn your astronomy.

I recall one evening at Pisgah state park. It was my first snow shoeing experience in the evening there in early winter by myself. Stars seemed so low in the sky, so close to me, bright and sparkling, almost winking at me. On the way out, I heard a bird and turned off my flash light, looked up through the branches and saw the stars, dancing, putting on a show through the trees and above the trees, amazing WOW.

Communicating with me.
Always look up and around.
What do the stars mean to you?

Rainbows

Rainbows are a combination of water and light. Raindrops and seven differently colored wavelengths of sunlight - red, orange, yellow, green, blue, indigo, and violet. When sunlight passes through the raindrop at a certain angle, the white sunlight separates into the different colors.

Appreciate the colors and its beauty. Thank you for the sight.

From a very early age we are taught the folklore of finding treasure at the end of the rainbow.

Thunder and Lightning

I can listen and watch thunder and lightning for hours. They are occurring for evenings at a time.

What causes it?

Usually signifies a change in the temperature.
Welcome in the new day.

Appreciation of the Elements

Appreciate and spend time in all seasons outside, all times of day, all weather.

Do you love rainbows and stars as I do? The earth, the air, water and fire?

Walk, acknowledge and pray each day.

I have placed many things in my home to appreciate the four elements. Air: Rattles, incense, wind chimes. Water: waterfalls. Fire: candles and wood stove. Earth: crystals and stones, a favorite beach weathered stone as a door stop. Hanging plants and ivy everywhere, surrounding my bed and walls in a sunny bedroom. Bring Nature into your home. This will help you connect with the elements of Nature.

Lastly, it is our sacred responsibility to respect all elements, all life on earth. We do this by,

Recycling, composting, use nature based products, less pollution of air and water. Conservation of lands and water.

Peace within.

Chapter 6

Recognizing Energy

Lets begin by discussing ways we experience energy in every day life. We might not realize it but we see it, hear it and feel it.

We see it when:

We see our own breath when we breathe out into the cold air.

We see the hot steam rise off our body during exercise in the cold weather.

We see heat rise from the hot pavement in the summer.

We see heat and steam rise from a heated iron or pan of water on the stove, especially when the room is cold.

We see the flames, sparks, heat and smoke emit from a fire.

We see the current above the high voltage wires running between the telephone poles.

We see bolts of lightning or a tornado in the sky.
We see a whirlpool and the force of water behind it.
We hear it when:
We hear our heartbeat.
We hear the vibration or buzzing of electricity.
We hear the sound of a river bounce off ledge behind us, hearing it twice.
We feel it when:
We feel a hug that feels good.
We feel goose bumps when we are happily surprised or horrified.
We feel the hot sun warm our bodies.
We feel the wind against our face and body.
We feel the tingling between our hands.
We feel our muscles relax when receiving a massage.
We feel the sexual energy and/or love between one another.
We feel the bad energy or anger or pessimism of another.
We feel the positive energy or joyfulness or enthusiasm of another.

"Each day we shift our energies to meet our daily trials, responsibilities and obligations. We learn early in life when and how to smile, when to be serious, when to be studious. We have learned what activities and postures make us more or less vulnerable. It is a matter of controlling and utilizing our energy to the fullest to meet whatever the life situation requires us to do." (24)

Now we must train our minds and eyes to see, hear, and feel this energy more. Let's begin by talking about our energy, our chakras and how they interact with the energy around us. Each of us have an aura, energy field made up of our own physical, mental, emotional and spiritual selves. In other words, what are we thinking and what we are feeling influence the energy fields around our bodies. Simply put, we are told that we have seven major chakras from head to toe described differently depending on who you talk and listen.

The base chakra is located at the base of the spine and associated with the earth and our will to live.

The sacral center is located at our sexual organs and determines ones' sex drive and life force.

The solar plexus is located between the naval and sternum and is associated with healing, intentionality, and connected place within the universe, human connectedness.

The heart chakra is located just above the heart and our love flows through it to all life.

The throat chakra is located in our neck associated with communication and taking responsibility for oneself especially our spiritual growth.

The forehead chakra is located in the middle of the forehead between our eyebrows. It represents our wisdom, insight and awareness. I believe this aspect allows one to be in a flow, control what's happening or about to happen.

The crown chakra is located on top of our head and related to the person's connection to his spirituality. When open, it creates an peace and faith, and a sense of purpose in our lives. (25)

Writing this book is one of my life's purpose.

Concentrate on the chakras. Understand and learn the chakra energies about yourself and you present an opportunity to merge them with Nature's energies. More importantly, we can connect to other planes or dimensions when in the right place and right time.

To learn more, I suggest reading The Hands of Light by Barbara Ann Brennan.

Physiologically, our heart and brain allow us to connect with the earth energies. In short, our heart interacts with the rhythms of the earth and then exchanges that information to the brain. The heart and subtle energies are not bound by space and time. Our mind and its beliefs based upon our past experiences may not give us the space we need to be open to new experiences (26) For example fear based thoughts get in our way. Angry emotions may get in our way.

There is a way to bypass the system I just described. The mind works mainly through the higher frequencies of the brain. When we want to tap into any source other than our mind, we need to be connected with the heart and with the lower frequencies of our brains. When we want to connect with the subtle energies of Earth, we need to be in a similar state of being. I believe that we need to be thinking less and more open to our hearts.

I believe there are other planes of existence. We connect to these planes or dimensions by raising our vibrational levels of our energies. Many times, our emotions (fear) can block the flow of energy in our chakras. These emotions can be easily released in Nature.

If you want to connect with the spiritual dimension then you must open your crown chakra. (27)

Subtle energies are all energies that are not electromagnetic in Nature. Electromagnetic energies comprise of only .005 percent of the total matter/energy of the universe. Therefore, the majority of existing energies are subtle energies. Life force energies also called chi, prana …are an important aspect of subtle energies. We can go weeks without food, days without water, minutes without air, but only seconds without life force. Our health can be defined by the flow of life force through our different body systems. Life force is found in plants and animals and in Earth herself.

Even more complex….

There are many subtle energy systems connected with the earth. All of these systems consist of these components: a field, grids, and connecting vortexes. The fields are information systems that are located in layers around the earth. These layers vary in width and frequencies. The grids are networks of energy lines that we find on the surface of the earth. We use the energy found in the grids on the earth and potentially connect to the human consciousness in the third-dimensional reality in the field, a layer above and around the earth.

Vortexes are the connections between the fields and grids. Vortexes are spiraling connections between the two systems, allowing the exchange of energy and information between these two systems. Vortexes vary in diameter and length, tens of feet to hundreds of miles. Meaning that you can connect with subtle Earth energies basically anywhere.

Let the energy flow through you in Nature.

Society controls most of the energy and our energy. Better, to go to Nature, the natural environment rather than the man made environment. We are more grounded in Nature. Everything in Nature has energy. The circle of life and its sacred flow of energy. The interconnectedness, the energy.

It is easier to connect to subtle energies in Nature, less distractions. Jaap Van Etten says that we are often attracted to places that make us feel good. "These places have a certain combination of energies that are important for you in that moment. They will offer experiences that will support you. They are often centers of vortexes. He suggests that we connect through meditation. Connecting to your heart from a place of love, connecting with Earth, connecting with the universe, and connecting with the energies of the vortex (or sacred place) where you are sitting for your highest good. This means that you intend to connect only with those energies that support changes and transformation that move you toward experiencing a joyful, happy spiritual life filled with love and abundance in this physical reality. " (28) You are already familiar with my favorite posture/meditation. I suggest reading more books associated with meditation if you require more help maintaining your own energy and space, a good place, a happy place.

Our heart is one such vortex that pumps blood throughout our body, pumps energy and life into us. The vortex of the heart is "the region of the apex of the heart where muscle fibers of the ventricles make a tight spiral and turn inward." A vortex.

A sacred site is a place where an ancient structure exists or a place that had been used for ceremonies over long periods of time, like caves, springs, and mountains. Experiences at these sites differ greatly depending on the spiritual development of the person.

We are surrounded by energy. Every transformation of energy and matter uses energy. The process of photosynthesis is when a plant transforms carbon dioxide and water into sugar and it uses energy from the sun. When animals eat that plant, they gain energy from it and they use energy in finding and eating the plant. Evaporation is when water (as we see it) warms and transfers to a vapor (which we do not see). Water can freeze and transfer to snow and ice (as we see it). Burning wood will release the heat and light it used to grow before it was cut into firewood. Energy moves in all directions just as the wind blows as they say. Energy moves in the vortexes as well.

The first time I saw energy in Nature was after spending a few days on the Long trail. An early morning mist and sunlight breaking through at the same time. I sit quietly, resting on a rock upon a mountain vista. I originally squinted my eyes. I focused softly in front of me and saw my first image of energy. Immense, drifting towards me, a white or hazy cloud dispersed, enveloping me. Yes, we are often surrounded by energy. Wow. We just don't see it.

Thereafter, most of my initial experiences occurred either near or over bodies of water. At rivers, waterfalls, and ponds. Then my experiences expanded to other places in Nature where I intended to see it, hear it and feel it.

I also read and learned as much as I could about our own energy fields and the energy around us. I am still learning to this day. Most notably, energy flows where our attention goes. Pay attention to the energy moving in your body and around you.

Rivers

I have two favorite places along the West River.

how I developed a relationship with nature

Story #1

The first, a vortex described as my "Favorite Place" in Chapter 1: The path narrows and slightly ascends to a fifty foot plateau.

I can always feel the breeze and cooler air. The initial ledge begins at twenty-five feet to as high as 75 feet. Water drops off the moss covered ledge on my right and no shoreline exists below me on my left. The path might be twelve feet wide and descends vertically twenty-five feet to the river. Fewer trees exist on the ledge side but there are enough from both sides of the path to maintain the canopy above me.

Mountains to my east, west and north and densely populated hemlocks in all directions enclose this space. Yet everything appears expansive when you look away from this small place.

I look across at the river. The river just comes at you here. Water enters this area from streams on both sides of the river. Whirlpools then swirl amongst the rocks and the rushing water form the oncoming rapids.

The river rushes into this spot and veers off in another direction while the cooler breeze, sound and energy is left to bounce off the ledge behind me and whomever is in is path. And for those aware of it, a certain amount of energy may flow through you.

My ear towards the river, hears the river. My ear away from the river, hears the river, as a reflection off the ledge. Much like hearing a car behind you on a busy street, you hear several cars approaching you, some from the front, some from behind. The sound can be enhanced when wearing a hood as I was this day (like a sea shell hears the ocean, I hear the oncoming rapids)

Story #2

And the second, a vortex described as "My Meditative Place" in Chapter 1:

This a section of the river is where Cobb Brook runs into the West River. We have a very highly charged area where the brook and river connect with its respective flowing waters and energies. We have mountains, higher than ever before on this path. Mountains to our left and mountains to our right. The Ball Mountain Dam sits one quarter mile up the river, hidden from view by landscape. The dam stands 265 feet high and 915 feet long, holding back almost eighteen billion gallons of water for flood control purposes. Yet permitting a consistent flow of water year round.

All waters and energy are funneled into this space. To me this is the most charged area on this path. Actually, one of the most charged areas I have ever been, secluded in Nature. Yet I always become grounded and balanced here. Initially, this was my favorite place in Nature, a place I was attracted to, a place that feels good. (29) Now this is a vortex.

I gaze over the river, visualizing the vibration energy coming off the water. Yes, I can see the energy. It looks something like the heat rising off the hot summer pavement or the electrical energy rising above the power lines at times. Or better yet, it closely resembles the fuzzy screens on the old black and white television sets, only not as fuzzy?

Energy. I welcome that energy into my body. I lean forward and stand in front of the park bench. I close my eyes. I motion it towards me by extending my arms out slowly, palms pushing away, and curling my arms back towards my chest slowly, palms facing me. Four more postures follow. (I'll describe this meditation fully in Chapter 10) . I repeat this action several more times, slowly and deliberately. Reciting my personal mantra all the while. A prayer. I open my eyes when I can feel the tingling of energy in my fingertips and the sensation throughout my entire body, from head to toe. My crown chakra is open. I feel balanced. I am now totally relaxed. My energy and mind in a good place. Very far from man made inventions. In commune with Nature.

Many times alongside these locations in the river and at different vantage points, I stop and face the river. Arms extended, palms up.... Instantly in the moment. White clouds, sometimes small opaque clouds close in above my forehead. Two arm movements and I feel the energy moving. Starting with energy to the fingers, very heavy energy on the fingers. I can move my hands and feel the energy attached and moving along with them. At times, a steady stream of energy coming and leaving my head. Much energy in the air, see and feel it. Prana. Changing colors, settling down thru my head, white and gold light. The river becomes quiet.

One time, I see three human sized auras over the river

Two more stories follow:

Story #3

I can remember a November walk along Connecticut river where I stopped at a waterfall. Cupped and splashed the waters on my forehead. I saw the sun passing thru trees and stared up at the setting sun, close to mountains and beyond. I saw the energy between sun and myself - actual heat between the cold air. I felt the area behind my back and throat open up to the energy. Gave thanks to the universe for my experience, growth and fun and relationships.

Story #4

Another time at Pisgah State Park, I read and meditated at ponds edge. The water breaking lightly against rocks and shoreline logs. Quiet. I open my eyes to spirit eagles - long, expansive wings. Blocks of energy moving above the pond. I meditated and prayed more. I cited my Nature prayer and the wind picked up. I expressed my thanks. I saw us as one looking out over the water and sky. These time outs (in Nature) are high vibration level moments and appear enhanced when I am alone. I am more sensitive and experience a higher feeling.

Remember when your mind is clear, it is possible to go beyond the five senses. Rest peacefully and focus on the natural surroundings. Again, energy flows where your attention goes. Pay attention to the energy moving in your body and around you.

I feel that two of the easiest ways to experience energy in Nature is when I see and feel the sun beaming down through my head, shoulders, arms, hands to my toes. I feel the heat and see the bright light when I close my eyes.

Another way is to touch and feel the new growth on small branches, swaying to the energy from my hands. Sense of touch, feeling the energy of branches, watching branches move with your energy. Its there for you to see with little effort.

Cave

As I reference later in Chapter 8, this area can best be described as a vortex, a clearly defined space that overlooks the valley straight out over tree tops into the sky. Ledge below it, ledge behind it. I could hear the gust of winds from the valley below, and feel the energy and breeze come through this space.

The cave is thought to be closely related to the symbolic heart and is often the place where the self and ego unite....symbolizing the search for the meaning of life, the maternal unconscious. Entering the cave is considered re-entry into the womb of Mother Earth.(30)

My energies align here. I become aware of how my body, mind, spirit come together. I feel the chi. I would lie on the floor of the cave, meditate and pray. I look over the forest, valley and sky at times and relax. It is here that I would hear and feel energy around me when I closed my eyes, meditating and praying. I always felt recharged. The vibration of the energy sounded like a soft humming and buzzing in my ears and felt like the hairs of my body stood on end.

Energies are around everything living in Nature. William J. Long talks about the sense of "presence" in his book (31). I interpret this reference to mean that animals and ourselves can sense the presence of another, perhaps their energy. Just a feeling? Unconsciously?

My energies play a part in it as do the four leggeds in this example of presence. I sat or lay many times in my cave when I sense someone below, hundreds of feet below. I would stand quietly and look down the mountain to see a deer walking along a ridge path, slowly and then looking up at me as well. Eyes locked. Perhaps, surprised to see me. This occurred a few times. Obviously a deer path. Obviously a sense of presence. And not a coincidence.

Not only do I recognize the presence of energy in Nature but I bring it home with me. I remember two experiences that had occurred after returning home from snow shoeing at the cave. Not only did I recharge my energy at the cave, I brought the spiritual energy home with me.

Story #1

One evening, I felt pushing on my shoulder while lying in bed. A light, energy, and warm tingling just kept coming thru my head and shoulders as I lie on my stomach, much like how they describe returning from an out of body experience but I had gotten out of bed just moments before. I sat up and experienced more coming in to my body. I meditated and asked what is going on here? No answer. I believe that my totems and spirits were returning with me from Nature as well. It sure felt good. I am often told that "the answer will come in time."

Its easy to understand how I might bring positive energy home with me. I exert myself climbing the ridges to the cave. Once there, I rest and recharge. I feel good about myself. I walk easily down the mountain and back home. Why not? Have you ever felt an infusion of energy into your body? Have you ever returned home feeling great? What happened that day? Something positive happened? Why are you feeling so good? Positive energy at play?

Story #2

Another evening, and I shared this meditation and prayer with my mom about bringing light to her before her surgery. Telling mom, there will be three angels supporting her before, during surgery and the recovery. She saw them in her home before the surgery. One on each side of her and one behind. I said the prayer from my heart, not rehearsed words or a practiced prayer, just from the heart. I feel a strong presence as I sit bedside. I prayed for courage, strength and any spirits to help her as needed or called upon.

My cabin became my go to place and my relationship with spirit evolved from there. Here my experiences were more visual and the vibration sound more intense.

Cabin

Again, unbeknownst to me at the time, I had selected a cabin site that I was attracted to, a place that feels good…a vortex, a highly charged area, secluded in Nature. A place where vibration essences serve as portals or doorways, to help you directly connect with a particular being, object, or place… Sitting on a cliff with a cliff behind it, the breeze and energy is left to bounce off the ledge behind me and whomever is in is path. And for those aware of it, the energy may flow through you. (32)

One story, I remember visiting my cabin for a few days…. I arrived at the cabin late morning. Partly sunny day. Birds, birds, birds. It had rained hard the previous week, waterfalls were running and the grounds were still soaking up moisture and small pools remained. For the most part, I puttered around the area of the cabin, measuring and thinking about the surroundings, not much but in the moment, no distractions, just the woods and the birds and the sound of the waterfall. I had prepared two marinated pork chops on the grill that evening and later laid down on the couch and watched a portion of a Kung Fu movie before the batteries in the dvd player lost their strength. I continue to rest and watch the sun fall closer and closer behind the trees and the mountain to the west. A sight to behold. It was around 830 900 o'clock when the sun barely set behind the mountain. I walked out to the deck facing the same west direction, trees, mountains, and sky. The waterfalls still running close by are still to be heard. It was noticeably different. No sun yet enough light and the absence of the bird song that I had heard all day. I cannot remember why I came outside but I felt it was a good time to do tai chi, be one with Nature in this moment and at peace. I perform the motions of tai chi and my feelings of energy flow as I face north. I am truly rewarded. Somewhere near the completion of my postures, I see a white cloud appear perhaps 15 to 20 feet in diameter surrounding me right there on the deck - its hard to describe the feeling - just feeling really special in the moment, appreciative, loved and a little WOW. Very much a part of the surroundings - harmony and peace and love with Nature. An aura, a cloud of energy surrounds me. A void, a cloud. Quiet, no birds. Seeing what appears to be a hazy or white dispersed cloud around and in front of you.

I learn the white cloud signifies purity, wisdom, and service.

I returned inside. I blend in here. I look out the windows, close my eyes, and hear a constant buzzing and ringing in my ears - a louder vibration. I am always aware of it.

Coincidently or not, I notice the Native American sand wall clock no longer works, it ticks but it stays on the second hand. It stays in the moment. So it will be.

Mountains

I was hiking a local mountain during a thunderstorm, not planned. I watched lots of lightning. It had just rained. Trees and ground wet. Very green. Everything green. I started sweating, it was very muggy. I saw lines of energy, no color. Then, I saw white circles, the size of softballs resonating from my head or above my eyes. It was overcast in the distance. The sun setting. I first see the details of trees far away, then the ridges, the mountains got bigger until they seemed right on top of me. I was emitting energy. Now, the white cloud surrounds me. My energies and Nature's energies, perhaps those of the charged thunderstorm merged together this day. I wouldn't recommend the thunderstorm mountain hike. Normally, wrong place, wrong time. This day was different.

Whether visiting my cave or cabin in the mountains, I exert energy in my legs and expand my lungs. I rest, meditate, pray, and recharge. I often feel in a different place when I leave this high ground to below. I feel suspended and floating, physically and mentally. Most times, I do not want to leave. I walk slowly and deliberately, enjoying the moment, investigating the wonders of the world around me.

Many years ago, I stopped and surveyed the last south ridge line. With little snow on the ground, I could see where a deer lay, facing the warm sun. I squat and touch the ground. I don't remember what caused me to put my ear to the earth. I could hear a beating sound. I listened again, same beating sound. Not a thundering sound of a truck or the nearby rushing river.

I believe that the heart beat of the earth aligned with my own heart beat. Synchronicity happens when ours resonates with the earth. Seeing out the same eyes, in tune, feeling same, in same moment.!!!! Things happen when both energies are aligned and present. Special experiences occur.

Lastly, the strength of prayer, whether here in the mountains, at the cabin or at the cave or at home, connects us to spirit (spiritual energies) in some way, sometimes, more profound than others. Like above and like below:

Upon nearing completion of this chapter, I saw a brief glimpse of my mom (thirty days past her passing). One evening I was lying in bed saying my prayers and sensed a presence in my doorway. I turned around to look and thought it might be my son, Kaden walking by to go to the bathroom but this figure was taller and remained only there a moment. It was my mom watching over me as I say my prayers just as she did while I was a child. A breath taking moment. A connection with Nature and Spirit make all these experiences possible.

Peace within.

Chapter 7

Power of Place

I would define a power of place in a simple way as a special place in Nature that makes us feel good. Our happy place. We know it feels good and we want more of it. We are attracted to it and keep coming back for more. Analytically speaking, a power of place is where we can restore the harmony and balance of our physical, mental, emotional, and spiritual self. Further, meaning, physically, it allows your body to rest and heal. Mentally, it allows you to clear your mind and solve life's problems. Emotionally, it allows you to find that special place in your heart. And spiritually, it allows you to connect with Nature and your spirit and God. A place that brings spiritual growth and wisdom to you. You'll know when you find it. Your "go to place " can change during and over your time. It can also provide many of qualities listed in some of the following examples. I apologize as I attempt to explain these qualities categorically, I might repeat some of my aforementioned experiences in doing so, and again describing my special places, the cave and the cabin.

A place where people might go to feel the presence of some vast, titanic power......

Monadnock Mountain, located in Jaffrey and Dublin New Hampshire, standing alone at an elevation of 3165 feet, commands the area around it in all directions. More than 100,000 people visit it each year and can seen by millions of people around New England. "If they have a difficult problem to deal with, they climb the mountain to clear their heads and make a final decision on the summit, where the stiff breeze and the wonderful view seem somehow to make it easier." Some observers think that Monadnock has such a powerful effect on people because it is literally a magic mountain. There are many who are convinced that it is. The native Abenakis saw it rising majestically above the rest of the landscape and assumed it was a powerfully spiritual place closer to the sun and the sky than anywhere else. The American Society of Dowsers have found invisible lines of power called "ley lines" on the summit, a power point where four and a half 12 foot wide lines cross. The Sioux conducted tribal ceremony on the summit. Christian writers call it a holy place. (33)

There are five paths to the exposed rock summit. There are many meditative spots and views on the climb and summit. Always winds but comfortable. The clouds and sky appear closer and have a presence.

Many shaman and monks would go to the mountains to seek guidance many times during their lives. The long vistas, the openness and vastness perhaps attracting them. I have learned that many Native Americans were more comfortable just below the tree line. I prefer the same but this one day, I ascended the summit where I could would experience the vastness as my own depth. In other words, in the scheme of things, me or some of my associated problems were relatively small. I still had strong emotions surrounding the welfare of my children. I felt a peeling effect as I sat facing the horizon. Something popped into my head. Everything is okay. What is, is. Other people share the same concerns during their lives, some better, some worse. I could do no more. A shift in awareness occurs. I was truly aware. I truly let go.

Mountains are the symbols for higher meditation, spiritual elevation, and communion with the blessed spirits….in linking heaven and earth. (34)

A place where it is a manifestation of Nature……

Caves, rivers, mountains and cathedral forests, are all manifestations of Nature and may carry a different spiritual perspective to you.

I have always found lakes, rivers, and waterfalls fascinating. Our bodies are made up of 90% water. We are often drawn to the waters.

"Water is always significant. It is the primal life source. It is constantly in transition, and it can reflect the same within your life. Water reflects our spiritual life and our emotions. Rivers are places where animals will gather to drink. Because rivers flow, they reflect a continual evolution and help you define the changing areas of your life and how to work with that process most effectively."(34)

I have sat on large rocks in the middle of rivers, basking in the sun with my feet dangling in the cold water, watching and listening to the flow of the water. I close my eyes, I meditate and open my chakras to the moment before me. I stand by the rushing waters to let go of my emotions and sit by the tranquil waters to calm my emotions.

A place where you enter a clearly defined space……

I can remember many years ago, hiking a portion of the Vermont Long trail one late Fall morning where I experienced stepping in and stepping out of the valley. I was disoriented and lost in the moment. I start by walking this mountainous path northbound for approximately 2 miles. I was prepared as most times, a backpack with overnight provisions and sleeping bag although this was an intended day hike. It was a forest setting. I immediately felt surrounded by life everywhere. I constantly hear the sound of running streams. It was misty and overcast. Chilly in that it began to flurry hours later on my way out. A roaring brook followed me for miles, up and down. Most of the leaves had fallen, however, there always seems to be that one beech leaf that draws my attention, blowing in the wind or slightest breeze, I will hear it, then see it. I continued at a very leisurely pace paying attention to my surroundings, enjoying the moment. Taking short breaks, focusing on views to my left, to my right, straight ahead, and behind me. Everything demanded my attention. I was lost in this moment. As I descended upon a valley, I could see that the brook flowed into it from the far right and sensed that the brook was no longer a part of this path. I decided to stop here and yes, dare I do it, meditate with miles to go ahead of me. I closed my eyes, listening to the water one last time, my legs standing spread apart and my hands at my side. I could visualize flames, intense flames. I concentrated more, what do I see? Are they flames? They appear to be more like bubbles, so intense, so real - colors changing from yellow, orange and white (my heart and crown chakra colors). I opened my eyes and saw that there was a ring of haze or slight fog around the rim of this valley. I thought I might be disoriented, I closed my eyes and looked again, sure enough a ring of haze. I started climbing the path. On cue, it begins to rain. I could see, hear and feel the rain drops. Further ahead, I stepped through the mist and the clouds and out of the valley. Suddenly it stops raining. I looked down upon the valley and it was completely fogged in. I felt like I had entered a lost moment of time or another dimension. Real or imagined, I was entering and leaving a clearly defined space.

    Another time, I can also remember walking along a Long Trail path, worn grounds below my feet, trees overlapping from the sides above me and the sun shining through at the end of the path, creating a sense of light at the end of a tunnel much like those described in near death experiences. I felt as though I was heading towards the light. Real or imagined, I was entering a clearly defined space.

A place where we can feel spiritual energy......

The more and more times I traveled to the cave and the more and more time, I meditated and prayed there...I began to honor this space. Every step was sacred, everything was sacred. An actual shift in consciousness occurs.

Aside from Nature, the first sacred place that comes to mind is the Church. A clearly defined place to worship and pray. A power of place where not likeminded people necessarily meet to worship and pray but like hearted people meet to worship and pray. Worship and prayer in unison creates a greater flow of spiritual energy.

A place where you can feel the natural rhythm of the earth......

I find kayaking the easiest way to feel the natural rhythm of the earth. I quickly become a part of the lake while gliding on local tranquil waters. It can become a more dramatic weekend/week long experience. I have kayaked days at a time in the Adirondack lakes watching shoreline wildlife and eagles perched or flying above me. I have literally drifted off in my kayak and mind, lost in the moment, only to be called back by another.

Likewise, I have kayaked north at the Connecticut Lakes and isolated ponds for a few days and had a difficult time acclimating myself to drive home.

A place where you blend into that environment or setting......

As discussed throughout this book, the more time I spent in the woods, the more quickly I would merge with Nature. Initially, it would take days to tune in to Nature, then it became hours, then thirty minutes, then fifteen minutes, then instantly. I returned to walk in the forest and wanted more of the same "feel good" feeling. I began to notice when that "get to know" time shortened. I appreciated it.

A place to relax, feel comfortable and safe, and meditate and pray......

These places, often for me, were dictated by my time, and the circumstances and priorities in my life. A place where I was afforded the privacy to conduct ceremony and prayer. Beginning in my home, the cave, the cabin, and the church. Most of my spiritual growth occurred in the cave and mountains and those experiences reflect that later in this reading.

A place where you are overwhelmed by the beauty in Nature......

Once upon a time I entered a "winter wonderland" on the Green Mountain trail. One Sunday morning after an evening snow and ice storm, I went for a mile or two snow shoe walk into the trail in the mountains. The snow was at least one foot deep and covered with a small layer ice. The sun was shining. A moderate twenty degrees and the snow had stopped falling earlier that morning. Fresh snow everywhere. All trees were wrapped in snow and ice, I could only see a portion of the tree and their brown under branches. The snow, wind and ice blanketed the trees. In particular, a smaller strand of pine trees in a clearing. Standing about ten feet tall and their delicate branches weighted down by the ice and snow, these pines looked like giant inverted snow cones. Every where I turned, snow cones. Every where I looked, white snow, a bright white ice. I could have easily been blinded by this solar snow eclipse had I not been wearing my sun glasses. The ice sparkled as did the little stars on the ground snowfall. I was overwhelmed. I had never been in such a wonderful place - a winter wonderland. Well, maybe, probably, probably many times as a child playing in the snow, rolling around in my snow suit and making snow angels. Hmmn. Everything remained white as I hiked out of the mountainous forest.

Sometimes we go to a favorite vantage point to watch a sunrise or sunset.

A call to leaf peepers and all, what about the fall colors?

A place where spiritual experiences or the unexplained happen......

Here, I have to share a spiritual experience that occurred at my cave and I can provide more details when it is described again under my power of place, the cave in this Chapter 8.

At the cave. It begins when I smudge. I look out over the river and valley and skyward above the tree tops as the light shines in upon me. I lay down on my woven blanket and bed of leaves. I recite my prayers. I am very relaxed, I begin to drift off. I meditate and welcome spirits into my life. I feel my crown chakra open and raise me. Surprised, I sit up for a moment, is this really happening? I lay down again and recite my mantra. I feel my head lift and my bandana slides and pulls away, and lifts away from my head. A shadow of a large bird passes over me as my eyes are closed. Leaves begin blowing in and out of the cave. Melting snow from above trickles on my face, stomach, and arms. I feel as though I'm being baptized by Nature this day.

A special place......

It could be a favorite place where you sit and lean against a tree, where you watch the sun rise or sun set over a mountain or the ocean. A place where you get your hands dirty in a garden. Really, any where outdoors, that carries a special meaning or feeling to you.

I would frequent a nearby walking path just across the Connecticut River from Brattleboro, Vermont. A five, ten minute walk and you're in the forest. I would venture down towards the river just far enough to remain unseen and undisturbed by others. A secluded space that overlooked the river. Where, I would lean against a large hemlock tree, watch and listen to the chipmunks and squirrels, and the chickadees and blue jays. Here, I sat to meditate and pray and meet my peace and silence for the day.

Your happy place.

A place where you spend a lot of time……

I walked the Jamaica State park path probably over five hundred times, some over night camping as well. I walked portions of the Long trail some fifty times. I hiked to the cave a hundred times or more. All of this time before the construction of my cabin. My cabin replaced a lot of time but will never take away from that time spent elsewhere. Eventually, you will have a complete acceptance of where you are. In all of these cases of familiarity, there appear high vibrations that you can see and connect to. It also stems from how you are feeling. A place you appreciate and are attracted to, you will have positive energy. The energy is magnified the more and more time you spend there.

A place where you have a sense of belonging, a sense of purpose……

Usually, a place you have been once before or many times before, perhaps as a child, a place enjoyed in youthful days. A secret fishing spot that served as your "alone time" for you and your father. A hunting camp. A favorite picnicking area for the family in a meadow, at a beach, or lakeside.

Going back, have been there before. Past growing experiences, continuing experiences, specifically spiritual ones. The mountains, rivers, and forests.

Spending an enumerable amount of time and experiences on my river walks, cave and cabin, with healthy and spiritual experiences and intentions, I naturally belonged here that served a purpose to grow spiritually.

Aside from Nature, a church with its sense of community and fellowship.

A place where you experience very intense feelings......

It can be as simple as a place where you might have walked with your children years ago. A mountain top where you got married. A special place that reminds you of interactions with close family and friends. A lakeside family reunion. A heart felt place.

Or a place in Nature where you might experience feelings you have never or rarely ever experienced before. I can remember exploring a secluded waterfall just a few hundred feet above and beyond a main pathway. I could actually sit and see oncoming walkers but they could not see me. All of my senses were fully engaged. I could see different colors red, yellow, and green as the sun lit up its waters. Simultaneously, I could feel the cold water running over my hands as my hands sink into the mossy, vertical ledge. I could hear the same waters from high above splashing the waters at my feet below. Smell the fresh mist and air from the waterfalls. A mindful, intense, engaged feeling in the moment. There is nothing else. Waterfall and me, one. Yes, I returned here.

A place where you see and feel
the energy of ancient peoples......

When I found how special the West River path was to me, I had to find out as much as I possibly could about this location. I visited the local historical society and read about the deaths from early

Native American battles. I also learned that there were several caves in the area where the tribes would retreat to safety at times. This led me on the adventure of finding this one place, power of place, the cave. My time spent at the cave illustrate just how special this cave and its surrounding lands were to me and the Native American ancestors. A shift in consciousness occurs and one can sometimes see and feel the energy of the ancient peoples. I didn't realize just how sacred a place this was until I began writing this book. I am honored and privileged to have seen and heard many things.

A place where you have a strong feeling to go to......

A place that you are beginning to visit on a regular basis and now feel an unexplained attraction. Much like a new boyfriend or girlfriend you are beginning to like or now love and want to spend more time. Good, great feelings and you want more. Sometimes, even a physical pulling.

I often had a strong feeling to walk my favorite river path, hike to my cave or visit my cabin. Almost as if fulfilling a need. My cave experiences that shortly follow will reference my feelings of growth and expansion, appreciation and love.

Perhaps, a physical need to recharge as well.

A place where you might retreat to rest and recharge your body, mind and spirit......

More than anywhere else, my cabin was not only my place to walk but became my place to reflect, read, relax and nap at times.

Shortly after a short walk to and around the cabin, a mile or so at least, I make a trip to the outhouse. Its almost as if my entire body relaxes and at that very moment I have to cleanse myself. I drink a lot of water here and feel as though I am purifying myself as well. A smudge and smudge of the cabin, cleanses myself even further. Mix in a tai chi

how I developed a relationship with nature

meditation and rest and my body has an extreme recharge makeover.

Many times I would arrive with the intention to do some outdoor chores and would only rest and nap for hours. I was just happy to be there, relieved to get there, slow down, sit back and take it easy. Relax and nap. A short walk in fresh air. A wood burning stove at times. Windows open with a stiff cool breeze. Sitting in a recliner or lying on the futon, warm under a wool blanket. Able to look out several windows and directions. Just let things happen rather make them happen.

I am physically recharged by my exercise and rest, emotionally by smudging my energies, mentally by my meditation, and spiritually by my prayer.

Many monks and shamans often retreated to the mountains to recharge their healing and spiritual energies.

Aside from Nature, a guys place. A man cave. Physically and mentally, a pool table in the basement. Spiritually, a place in your home where your heart lives without fear.

A place that remains hidden in the wilderness......

Generally, a place hidden in the wilderness separates a power of place from all others found outside of Nature.

Interesting, in that there are so many similarities between the cave and the cabin. Both locations sit up and back away, shielded by trees. Mountain and rock in front and behind. A cooler snow belt where it takes longer for the snow and ice to melt, always a cool breeze. Downright cold in the winter. Not an easy place to get to, both a difficult place to walk and snowshoe, challenging at times.

You are here with all Nature, in the middle of it, isolated from civilization. The streams and waterfalls, the sunsets and moon. The hooting bears, coyote, bob cat, deer, porcupine, turkey and birds of all kinds...Once you have arrived, you don't have to move very far to have it all. I'm one with Nature at this very spot.

I hear the vibration of energy at both the cabin and cave. I have experienced a higher vibration, higher frequency at the cabin. It sounds like crickets in a field but more constant and at a higher pitch. The vibration I hear at the cave and my home is more a constant buzz. Either way, I can feel the energy flow from my head to the toe at both places. Both a power of place and place of power. Definitely, places that restore the balance of my physical, mental, emotional, and spiritual self.

A place where energies converge, a vortex……

Only a few shaman went to the open spaces on the mountains, most went below the tree line. The cave and my cabin, both unintended, exist in similar places, both tucked away by the rocks and the trees.

The wind and energy both come towards these raised locations and the cliffs behind them with nowhere to go but back where they came from. Thus, the energy comes through those of us in that place and time. The sound can reverberate as well. All is heard here. All is felt here.

Aside from Nature, one of the best examples of power of place can the church. A cross symbolizing love and peace can serve as a link between the heavens and earth. A place where the like hearted people meet to worship and pray. Worship and prayer in unison creates a greater flow of spiritual energy.

A place we know thru our experiences and interactions……

A place where your experiences strengthen that relationship with Nature and spirit. I will now describe my two most powerful places in Nature, my go to places, the cave and my cabin, places where I experienced and continue to experience my most spiritual growth to this day.

Chapter 8

The Cave

Shortly after my experience on the river path, I investigated the history of this area through the local historical societies. I learned of the early inhabitants right along this river and valley, the Iroquois and the Abenaki Native Americans. The more I learned, the more I felt connected to the landscape. There were several caves in the area, some below and some above the dam. I was looking for a particular one called the pony cave. A cave and area where the Native Americans might retreat for safety many, many years ago. I traversed this mountain upside and down and sideways by myself until I found the cave. I discovered many nooks and crannies on this side of the mountain.

Many big rocks dumped by glacier lie in these valleys and hills, sit across and are very close to the river. Its a challenging walk at times, up and down mountain ridges, finally arriving after a 75 foot near vertical climb on all fours to the entrance of the cave. It sits up and tucked away, shielded by ledge and trees in the front and more mountain rock behind it. Making it even more difficult to find as you approach it from below is a shadow that conceals its opening. You will walk by it if you didn't know it was there. I actually found a smaller cave and retreat below before discovering this one.

Walking to the cave, I would always have to catch my breath, only until recently did I realize it was not my breath but my excitement that I had to contain, had to calm myself down.

I would travel here over one hundred times. Caves, rivers, and mountains are all manifestations of Nature, certain areas may carry more perspective to you - I came here to connect to the spirit. Native Americans and monks would go to mountains to seek guidance many times during their lives. Sometimes, just below the openness, just below the tree line. Such was the case here. The cave is located perhaps one hundred feet below the summit. I was more comfortable here as well. Only a few shaman went to the open spaces on the mountains, most went below the tree line. Others as described by Craig Brandon, "many people have climbed higher and used the summit as a meditative space when they have a difficult problem to deal with. They climb the mountain to clear their heads and make a final decision on the summit, where the stiff breeze and the wonderful view seem somehow to make it easier." (35). A greater flow of spiritual energy experienced here.

This area can best be described as a vortex, a clearly defined space that overlooks the valley straight out over tree tops into the sky. Ledge below it, ledge behind it. I could hear the gust of winds from the valley below, and feel the energy and breeze come through this space.

The cave is thought to be closely related to the symbolic heart and is often the place where the self and ego unite….symbolizing the search for the meaning of life…. the maternal unconscious. Entering

how I developed a relationship with nature

the cave is considered re-entry into the womb of Mother Earth.(30)

I developed a relationship with this power of place and my spiritual self through my interactions here. I will share my spiritual experiences and growth with you now.

I had found many smaller caves before I found this one. One cave in particular which I will call the lower cave from hereon out, was located just below this one. I was able to rest at this site before ascending vertically to "the cave." It offered a great sitting area outside and protection from almost three directions, an opening facing south, and large connected boulders to the other sides. The cave itself had a narrow entrance which would require you entering sideways from the west and even a smaller exit east, requiring crawling on your belly out. You could not stand inside but could possibly fit two or three adults hunched together. There was a small fire pit where others before me, likely local hunters had taken a break from the cold. Again, I had initially smoked cigars here and the smoke would exit north through an opening that was protected by other large rock adjacent to the outside sitting area. It was a great area to set camp.

One time, I met a hunter in the area who described how he saw a bear climb vertically up and over a nearby forty foot piece of ledge. He also watched me when I slid diagonally into a small crevice investigating a possible cave. I don't know who he thought was crazier, me or before me, the bear. I can't believe to this day that I crawled into some of the places I did on this mountain.

I have eight short stories to tell, describing how my relationship grew with my power of place, the cave.

Story #1

From my very first visit, I honored and respected "the cave". I crawled in from the south through a wide triangular opening with loose rocks and gravel sliding down behind me. I always investigated the smaller outlining spaces with a flashlight to make sure I was alone as coyote and other scat existed about. I could stand in the center as the walls were slanted towards center much like a tepee. There was a north rear exit that required crawling and climbing. I touched the ceilings and the walls of the cave. I sifted the pebbles and sand from the floor of the cave through my hands. I imagined those here before me. I was so thankful for finding this sacred place in Nature, in the mountains. I thought "what a go to place." My early ceremonies, again, believe it or not, involved smoking a cigar and watching the smoke climb as I prayed. I was probably here for two hours. I lay a red woven blanket on a bed of leaves, ate lunch and meditated by lying on my blanket, closing my eyes and reciting my special mantra. Yes, my very first vision was that of a larger than life Alaskan wolf - blue eyes and a heavy coat of fur. Perhaps, a mighty version of the four leggeds that inhabit the cave at one time. Although, I felt that this vision offered me protection, I was still anxious and ready to retrace my steps off the mountain while there was still daylight.

Years would follow when I was drawn here in all seasons and types of weather. Sometimes, I would take a day off during the week but I usually hiked in on a weekend. I can remember a July day when there was thunder, lightning and rain and I hiked as far as the lower cave. I sit back and listen to the rain here and feel the breeze. The forest was very green. The birds were singing and the creeks were running like the Amazon jungle. It was wet everywhere. I was drenched even in my wet gear. I said many spiritual prayers hiking in and out. This time I would ask for the alignment of my energy with a woman, spiritual oneness with Nature, and likely to make it off this mountain alive. I did not always hike all the way in to the upper cave. I felt very comfortable on this mountain, no matter where my journey brought me. I belonged here.

Story #2

One April day I left work early as I wanted to be here. It was a very sunny, 54 degree day. There was three feet of snow on the

how I developed a relationship with nature

ground, melting of course. Many birds were singing. I walked up the road maybe a half mile until I enter the woods and mountains on my right. Wearing winter gear, snow shoes and my back pack, my feet sink softly and quietly into the snow. Mostly a blue sky, some clouds. The streams are running. I see two deer go by as I rest at my first pine tree in the open meadow, ten minutes into my hike. Both deer paused. One moved. Then the other leaped as I moved. Lots of deer tracks , many fresh tracks. Where they lay on southwest facing ridge lines, feces. I eventually reach the lower cave in 1.5 hours, 3' of snow. Obviously, I paused at times too, like the deer. I saw an owl in its normal inhabited tree. I was in no hurry. Normally, I just rest at the lower cave before ascending to the cave. This time, I prayed, meditated, and chanted. I was very at peace. Very comfortable, probably very tired. A very tranquil setting, lots of white. I snow shoed back and forth sideways to reach the upper cave, however, the back entrance was covered by snow and I could not enter the front as well. I took a few moments to see and hear the river from here before traversing back down, sliding down 5 - 10- 15- 25 - 40' at a time. Upon leaving the hills and forest to civilization, I turn warm, my chest is warm, a comfortable warm feeling overcomes me. I feel loved.

Story #3

And yet another time, in late winter, I have a strong feeling to go to the cave. Approximately 18 inches of snow on the ground. A strong wind and sun. Blue skies with clouds. I wore a red bandana over my head and layers of clothes. Many times I stop and let my snowshoes sink and ground themselves into the carpet of snow as I perform my Tai chi postures. I arrive at the cave and I can hear and eventually see a deer in the valley below. I smudge cedar and sweet grass and lay down on my blanket. I repeat my prayers. Leaves begin to blow around me. A wonderful peacefulness, comfort, and cushion of energy surround my head. I thought I might leave my body. I hear chanting, see a white aura cloud around me. I hear the silence in between. I meet a teacher as I gazed out of the cave. There sitting around a camp fire, talking to me with his hands and finger, saying "what is, is. Abundance give away what you do not need, take only what you need (meaning to me, balance), continue to walk the path you are on." As I leave the cave, the wind is blowing so strong that I fear that some trees and branches may fall before me. The birds, every where are singing. I acknowledge many of them by saying hello. I began to learn and grow through common visions here. Quite often, answers brought with them, more questions. More wisdom, more questions.

Story #4

Another winter day, I retreated to the lower cave to recharge myself and restore the harmony and balance with my physical, emotional, mental, and spiritual self. I was surrounded by snow and ice and I could feel the water dripping from snow melt above as I sat just outside the cave. I could feel the sun shining through me, warming me, healing me, energizing me. I had recently fine-tuned one of my prayers thanking spirit for the light, warmth, strength and life force in my life, referencing the above aspects with the social norms of my life - family, friends, work, and community.

I recited my prayer here and shortly thereafter at a mountain stream overlooking the valley. I would hear the word "done" from above. I understood that I need not recite the prayer, it had been heard. I felt good as well.

Story #5

Over the years, I shared my special place and meditating experience with a few friends on the mountain and the cave. Most of which would involve smudging while there, reciting a few prayers, and they would hike higher to the top of the mountain while I stayed below in the cave. Sometimes, like this one day in March would be a longer meditation and ceremony with one. It was a fifty degree day. Snow, mud and water as we hiked in that day. We had lunch together in the cave. We smudged some home grown sage in a bowl, recited our prayers and intentions and meditated afterwards. I heard more buzzing in my ears than ever before. A very high vibration with a colleague of mine there. Up to three days after, I saw a bright star light in front of me, about one foot away from my right eye.

To no surprise, my friend wanted to return to the cave and we did so about a month later. Only this time, after we had lunch together, I descended down to the lower cave while he stayed behind, smudged his sage, and lay on his blanket, walking stick beside him and meditate alone. I planned to return one hour later. At the lower cave, I lay out my blanket, my back pack as my head rest, my staff on ground to my left, smudge and recite prayer. I hear an eagle as I chant my mantra. Upon completion of my prayer, I see rings of gold or a gold star off to my right side above my eyes. Later, I see and hear the eagle flying high in the sky above the river, partially in and out behind the obscured view of the trees. This was the first time I had seen an eagle here and felt that a connection had been made and I must return here. I did return and yes, I did see and talk to eagles here.

Story #6

On this Sunday in May, I was traversing the ridges to the cave, the mountain speaks to me. I had complete acceptance of where I was, here in the cave and here in my heart. I was glad to get here, and in no hurry to leave. I spent five hours that day, a slow pace in and a slow pace out, reciting many prayers. I lost my sense of time, only by looking at the daylight and feeling the change in temperature did I realize that it was time to go home from home. I stop and lay at my last ridge which faces the west and the setting sun. I feel a part of the ground and mountain as I lay with my ear to the ground. I hear the mountain speak to me. It sounds like rumbles, like winds passing through the earth of the mountain, like hoofed animals running upon the ground, or perhaps mother earth's heart beat. I have not heard the sound again to this day but will remember it forever.

Story #7

Real or imagined, not afraid. Home is where your heart lives without fear. Home, particularly when single, the cave was my home away from home, my retreat. It had been awhile since I visited the cave. This Spring day, I will welcome comfort and the spirits into my life. No snow on the ground, a bit muddy. I start out through the forests and hills as I normally do and will sense something at a distance, then it disappears behind the trees, following me at times, keeping an eye on me, protecting me, a bear (as I transcribe these notes, whenever I sensed a bear in the wilderness, more often than not, it would be off to my right even though I look left as well). Not afraid, I keep walking, This has happened before. Real or imagined. Not afraid. The colors seem to popping out today, brighter and closer than usual. I arrive at the cave and decide to explore further almost to the top of the mountain. Making my way slowly down the mountain I notice a bear hole in the side of the mountain, maybe a hundred feet away from the cave. Did I look inside? I attempted to climb to it but would slide backwards each time just as I was about to reach it. Real and not afraid, I returned to the cave. Upon entering, I hear a hawk nearby. I smudge. I lay down on my blanket and bed of leaves. I look out over the river and valley and skyward above the tree tops as the light shines in upon me. I recite my prayers. I am very relaxed, I begin to drift off. I meditate and welcome spirits into my life. I feel my crown chakra open and raise me. Surprised, I sit up for a moment, is this really happening? I lay down again and recite my mantra. I feel my head lift and my bandana slides and pulls away, and lifts away from my head. A shadow of a large bird passes over me as my eyes are closed. Leaves begin blowing in the cave and out. Melting snow from above trickles on my face, arms and stomach. I feel as though I'm being baptized by Nature this day.

how I developed a relationship with nature

Story #8

One can see how my vibration might be raised here. The wonder and excitement, and here home alone. I visited the cave this one day in March. Snowflakes are falling. As normal, no one knows my whereabouts. I was alone with my provisions, (prepared to stay the evening) and my painted walking stick. This day I was very aware and in tune with my surroundings. I was able to focus with more attention. The land and the sky, the snow, and the birds in trees. I could look beyond and focus in on the snowflakes in the distance, zooming in, very aware, very close, a part of it. I recognize a sense of closeness and connection. "Objects appear closer and have a presence, jump out at me and demand attention." (36) I smudge, I meditate and pray. I invite the spirits into my life. I correct myself and white light myself and invite friendly, loving, and teaching spirits into my life. I received cloudy visions, asked for clarity but only heard chanting voices. I felt vibrations inside of my ankle up to my thighs - just as if a doctor was holding his vibrating metal instrument against you.

I maintain a heightened awareness, a closeness, and connection as I leave the cave. My muscles are relaxed and my body feels a sense of lightness. I move effortlessly, floating with the snowflakes. I blend in with the snowflakes and its surroundings. The water and streams are talking to me and I listening to them. I am one with Nature. This is a special place, a sacred place, my place of worship. I had not attended church in decades.

The more time and more familiar I became with my surroundings, the stronger my feelings and the stronger, my sense of place. I learned that it stems from how you are feeling. A place you appreciate, a place you are attracted to, a place you belong. My positive energy multiplies and I feel and hear the higher vibrations here. I feel the energy flow from my head to the toe and hear the energy in the ground and air.

Over the years each time I return, nothing has changed, maybe a fallen tree or two, less saplings. Still tracks, still streams, still big rock, still paths leading up and down the ridge lines. Once I enter the forest and mountain and air. I can breathe, relax. I have not really encountered many, once a hunter, once a group of friends. Otherwise, always quiet. Only my heartbeat. I am very open to the surroundings and the circumstances to be presented here. I recognize the same rocks, crevices and formations that act as land marks on my way to and from the cave.

After many travels here and the purchase of over 120 mountainous acres in a nearby town, my focus shifted from the cave to a secluded cabin.

Peace within.

Chapter 9

The Cabin

I awaken from thirty minutes of meditation and prayer to birds whistling and flying around each of my cabin windows. I rise to my feet to look out every window to see dozens of chickadees fly by each window and feed on the partially snow covered ground. Whistling and chirping all the while. Then, within a few minutes, they fly away.

Someone appreciated my prayer. My thoughts focused upon the protection our mountains, specifically the largest proposed wind turbine project in Vermont and all mountains where large corporations attempt to build wind turbines and upon the protection of our waters, specifically the Standing Rock Sioux protest and all waters where large corporations pollute of our waters for a profit.

Iberdola Renewables Corporation promised the towns of Grafton and Windham, Vermont 1.5 million dollars annually, some of the cash would be allocated in the form of direct partnership payments to be doled out to residents to spend as they wish. The corporation attempted to buy votes but the communities said no to the turbines.

Energy Transfer Partners with the government support of the Trump Administration, however, complete the Keystone pipeline which crosses the Missouri River and Native American ancestral burial grounds, risking contamination of drinking water and damage to sacred burial sites.

What a powerful place my cabin came to be over the increasing amount of time I spent there, the prayers and the ceremony, and the meditation and the tai chi practiced there. My cabin unexpectedly replaced my cave as my go to place in the mountains. One should not be surprised. They have striking similarities.

I bought 123 acres on a mountainside in southern Vermont approx 30 minutes from Brattleboro. When the opportunity to build a permanent residence did not materialize, I decided to build a cabin to enjoy the outdoors as my time allowed.

Little did I know at the time, I was attracted to a place where mountains are symbols for higher meditation, spiritual elevation, and communion with the blessed spirits. (34). I spent nearly a year walking the entire property, following old logging roads, looking up and down ridge lines, scouting intertwining paths until I located the perfect cabin site. I happened across the site in late Fall and was able to carry two wooden Adirondack chairs ½ mile through the forested hills before the snowfall. I sat there at times imagining sitting on a deck or in a cabin enjoying the view in all directions. They say location, location, location is everything. I found mine and built a cabin the following spring and summer.

The cabin sits up and away, shielded by trees and mountains behind it. The ridge is approximately forty feet wide with another forty feet gradually sloping behind it. Cliff and rocks and ledge above and below, forty feet ascending and descending each way. The cabin and cliff side deck overlook a valley to the west and below, and

how I developed a relationship with nature

the mountains above and beyond it. Little did I know, it lies on a snow belt. With it, cooler summer breezes at times and heavy long lasting snow at others.

An abundance of wildlife, sometimes can be seen or heard. Raptors and eagles ride the air currents in the distance to the west. Occasionally, a barred owl flies low amongst the trees and deck at sunset. Sometimes, a residing bobcat appears, above, cliff side. Raccoons, turkey, deer, moose, coyote, bear, and fisher cat have been spotted nearby and frequently tracked here. Mice, chipmunks, and squirrels. Grouse, woodpeckers, and many other birds as well.

Mountain streams and waterfalls can be seen and heard out of the north facing windows. While more ledge and forest face south and east. Sunset to the west disappearing over the mountains. The full moon bringing light from behind and over us at times

Tall hemlocks and various hardwoods grow along the ledge and ridge line. I removed as few trees as possible. Just enough light and air come through the canopy. Two mighty oak trees stand on the front sides of the cabin. Which brings us to the story of "Bimadisiwin" and my name for the cabin.

Bimadisiwin is written by Blackwolf Jones and means:
To live life to the fullest. To live the good life.

His story describes how the acorn grows into a sapling then the mightiest oak by trusting Nature and the Universe. Much like we should. To learn more details about this lesson and more teachings from Blackwolf Jones, I refer you to the book "Listen to the Drum". (37)

Generally, an oak tree was a place where family or council would discuss life issues.

I would often hug these oak trees upon leaving my cabin and feel the warmth and strength they provided me.

The approach to the cabin presents a challenging walk from a logging road and better yet, the main road way (a ½ mile of ascending logging paths improved by my son, John and his equipment, Thank you John). The cabin remains partially hidden by trees, saplings and branches as you approach it from below. You will walk by it if you didn't know it was there.

Initially the cabin was fourteen by twenty feet (280 square feet) but with additions, now stands at fourteen feet by forty feet (560 square feet) built upon layers of cinder blocks carried two hundred feet by hand. Pressure treated beams and thick plywood form the base of the structure. Many windows, including four foot by six foot wide sliding windows, three on the west side overlooking the cliff side valley and two facing the north side streams. Warmed by a corner woodstove and cooled by strong cross breezes.

The cabin frame is constructed by 2 X 6 pine boards and horizontal ship lap pine on the interior and exterior walls, floors and ceilings. Stained by clear polyurethane inside and a light oak stain on the outside. All coated two or three times to preserve the cabin finish to this day. The roof is finished by a green sheet metal that also extends out from the west door of the cabin to provide a clear and dry surface upon entering the cabin. The full length pressure treated deck still requires some replacement from the forest dampness. A waist high railing was installed along the entire deck (except for its north and south entries) to protect one from accidentally falling cliff side.

A small wood pile and a portable generator lie on the deck, roof covered, and opposite the cabin door. Peace wind flags and battery strung white lights embrace the upper beams.

As you enter the cabin on your immediate left, a coat rack hangs above a small rectangular table. Immediate right, a linen cabinet which stores towels, linens, paper products, first aid and other emergency accessories. Cross country skis, a broom and axe stand in the corner.

Next left, a Navajo decorative sand painting clock with various designs symbolizing healing, hangs above a 36 inch folding oval table and two chairs that look out a 48 inch sliding glass window to the deck, valley below, and skyline above.

how I developed a relationship with nature

A corner wood stove and a large old pair of leather strung snow shoes are fastened high to the adjacent wall and could be used in a pinch.

Strings of white lights surround the east and west facing windows and the entry way into the north addition room.

A traditional design shield representing the eagle society of the Ojibway tribe is secured above the entry way as well. The shield is half red/ half dark blue with the eagle centered half blue/ half white respectively, turkey feathers attached, hang below it. Representing war and peace, I am told.

You face three sets of eagle curtains as you enter the naturally lit additional room. Left facing, a narrow coffee table with guide books, magazines and a small flat screen tv upon it. A single bed beside the north facing 48 inch windows. A large peace flag representing world peace in many languages decorates the far wall. An exit is in the far corner and some firewood and kindling in a wood rack nearby.

As you turn around and walk through the main cabin again, a large 8 X 11 hunter green tapestry rug adorns the floor. A dream catcher is suspended above a pull out futon couch. The mattress and pillow covers are decorated with a forested landscape theme of pines, bears, moose, wolves…. A pair of old bamboo fishing poles and net affixed to the wall the above.

My personal totem figurines are placed in window sills, representing their directions, the bear north, the deer south, the mountain lion west, and the eagle east.

A loft above two dressers with a small wooden ladder and stool beside it. Many books referencing topics from native american stories and ideologies, Nature, chakras and energy and religions and beliefs are stacked upon the dressers (approaching two hundred books at any one time). Extra blankets and two mattresses lie above. A wooden woven waste basket and linen hamper lie beside the dressers.

A Native American hatchet peace pipe on a south wall above the entry way to the kitchen demonstrates the willingness to accept peace to live together or the willingness to fight to protect ones land and values. The framed "Bimadiswin" story is mounted just to the right of it.

A white kitchen angel hangs in southwest corner of the kitchen. A condensed space, 8 X 10, holds the following: a propane gas stove, kerosene and battery lamps sit upon the kitchen counter. A six foot tall propane refrigerator adjacent in the corner. A tool box. A small propane oven and cooker, two small dressers filled with pots and pans, dishes and utensils. Some staple foods and spices are stored below in plastic containers in the counter cupboards. A detailed trail map of the property, a winter sky view picture, and calendar decorate the walls. Several blue metallic coffee mugs are secured to wooden pegs above two of the smaller sliding glass windows (20 x 36). A 20 x 48 sliding glass window faces south is located above the kitchen counter top with its storage below.

A green upholstered revolving recliner that normally faces north towards the wood stove and the addition sits front and center. A small sitting stool normally nearby to place items upon while sitting.

Back outdoors again. An open outhouse, one hundred feet upwind, on a nearby cliff, looks across at the mountains. Enclosed on three sides, waist high, and a roof above it. Otherwise wide open.

An open outdoor shower is located forty feet away and visible from the kitchen window. Framed pressure treated corners with a plastic fabricated floor and drain. Open ceiling and walls. Usually, a very cold water shower unless previously heated by a black bag and the sun.

A large open wood shed with a tarp covered roof closer by, stores firewood and outdoor tools.

A metal iron fire pit with a screen cover lies down hill, thirty feet north of the addition.

Its normally a very wet spring , a very green summer, a very colorful fall, and a very white cold winter.

How did my cabin became a power of place?

how I developed a relationship with nature

1. Naturally, the location. I chose a place that provided the overlook to the valley, the mountain views, and tucked away amongst the trees and rocks. Cliffs below and cliffs behind it. Cathedral hemlocks and other big trees.

Caves, rivers and mountains are all manifestations of Nature and may carry more perspective to you. Placed in the middle of the forest and mountains, this location reminds of Mount Monadnock with lots of ledge and rock and its closeness to the sky. The big difference, its more secluded and private.

The surrounding property offers comfortable walks on the soft ground of pine needles, moss and tall grasses. And a choice of gradual or steep paths.

Sunshine or shade. I can hear the gust of winds from the valley below. At times, the swaying branches can sound like pounding rains coming your way.

A place where I could eat the native black berries and raspberries and the planted blueberries and apples.

Although I was a half mile or more away from the main road and in the mountains, I always felt safe and a part of Nature here. I blended into this environment and would remain undiscovered here.

Most importantly and unbeknownst to me at the time, I had selected a cabin site that I was attracted to, a place that feels good…a vortex, a highly charged area, secluded in Nature. A place where vibrational essences serve as portals or doorways, to help you directly connect with a particular being, object, or place… Sitting on a cliff with a cliff behind it, the breeze and energy is left to bounce off the ledge behind me and whomever is in is path. And for those aware of it, the energy may flow through you. (38)

Connected and committed. The cabin is "my go to place" to restore the balance of my physical, emotional, mental, and spiritual self.

I physically invested time locating (traversing the mountain) and building cabin, walking and working the surrounding property. I connected with the cabin from the ground up. My hands in the soil, pouring sand, laying the foundation cinder blocks. I improved the views of the cliffs, the valleys, the sky, and mountains beyond even from the outhouse by cutting trees and brush. I maintained the trails. I added blueberry bushes and apple trees and at times, a garden.

I developed a strong sense of place by improving the landscape and spending time here to reflect and relax.

I purified myself here. I always drank a lot of water. I often felt as though my body was cleansing myself with many trips to the outhouse at times.

2. Emotionally I brought my own energy into the home. I decorated the cabin with my selected totems, Native American made items, and peace flags. I spent more time here than I previously spent at the cave. I was able to read, reflect and relax. I felt comfortable and safe, I could focus without interference and apprehension.

I enjoy my time at the cabin. I love the cabin. My positive emotions and attraction magnify my energy here. I feel the chi around me. I can hear it as well, a higher frequency that sounds like crickets in a field. I recognize and appreciate the complete silence. At home, it was a steady, lighter buzzing sound at times. Here, more constant.

3. Mentally, it is a place to recharge and give my mind a rest as well. They say, home is where your heart lives without fear. A retreat to solitude. I was so relaxed at cabin, I would do little work at times because I was just happy to be here, relieved to get there, slow down, nap, sit back and take it easy. Pure enjoyment. Its all here. I don't have to move very far to have it all. I'm with one, right at this very place. At times, all of my senses were engaged. I would look around out the windows at the green trees and cover, the blue sky, listen to the swaying trees, waterfalls and singing birds. Smelling spring, smelling fall, feeling the winter cold. Hear the wind and feel the breeze. I have no concept of time only a sunrise, sunset, morning or evening chill signify a change.

how I developed a relationship with nature

4. Spiritually - Like the cave, I was able to focus on my spiritual growth at the cabin. I honored my home by smudging/cleansing it and myself often and by spreading tobacco around its perimeter. Everything is sacred. I recited many prayers both religious and Nature here. I meditated with my postures and could feel and see higher vibrations at times. I could feel energy flow from my head to my toes. In turn, enhance the flow of my spiritual energy around me.

I often viewed the cabin as my church, my sacred place. I had a sense of belonging and purpose.

You begin to grow and learn at power of place, acquire wisdom, acquire answers through our experiences and interactions. More answers, more questions. I have done that here.

I cannot speak enough of how blessed I am to have found my power of place. A place to go…Just today, after praying for all of Nature, their habitat, our environment…Surprise! Just as my prayer ends, I hear a chickadee chirping outside my cabin screen door. I turn left, it is looking directly over at me, eye to eye, chirping away as it walks along a row of firewood stacked on my deck.

Minutes later, I remain looking left but facing more north out an adjacent window and I see small black bird learning how to fly perhaps for first time. My view is framed in by the deck. It flies just past the outreaches of the deck, above cliff side, back and forth, just high enough between the trees and disappears moments later. It must reside in a nearby nest or a birdhouse on either end of the deck. Each day, brings with it, something new.

The cabin and cave have striking similarities.

Only a few shaman went to the open spaces on mountains, most went below the tree line. The cave and my cabin, both unintended, provided the overlook, the mountain views, and tucked away amongst the trees and rocks. Both had cliffs below and behind. Long vistas, big trees, and located below the tree line. And most importantly, a true vortex.

I searched both long and hard to find both my cabin location and the cave. I spent a lot of time meditating and praying at the cave and continued to do the same at the cabin.

Again, the approach to the cabin and cave could be challenging at times and the destination made easier. "Many when they have a difficult problem to deal with, they climb the mountain to clear their heads and make a final decision on the summit, where the stiff breeze and the wonderful view seem somehow to make it easier." (39)

Peace within.

Chapter 10

Enhancing your Relationship with Nature

You might recognize some of my thoughts from previous readings but they are worth repeating again and again, here and now and always. I'll end with my prayer, its most recent revision.

I remember my prayers at age three, kneeling at my bed side with my brother, in flannel pajamas, my hands clasped together, elbows leaning against the bed, and my head bent forward. Our mom and dad stood just outside our door. I said them aloud. Mom says I would thank God for everything and everyone even the trees and green grass. At one point I told my parents I was old enough to say them by myself.

Prayers change as we grow, prayers repeated with these changes, carry more meaning. Prayer words carry a lot of meaning, and come from the heart whether they are recited at bedside, church or in Nature. Say your prayers and you will enhance your spiritual relationship with your God and Nature. Repetition breeds familiarity with Spirit so much so that occasionally, I would hear Spirit say "done" when I had only begun a portion of my prayer. I'd attempt to pray again, "done." Now, I have learned to listen once.

Meditation and prayer calm the mind and reach out for that higher connection. One must conduct all with honorable intention when seeking answers.

It is important to express our gratitude and thanks. We can show our gratitude by respecting mother earth. Use natural cleaning products, recycle, composting, and don't waste. Do not harm the earth.

Welcoming Nature into your home. Hanging plants in living room and bed room and porch. Installing a small ceramic based rock waterfall in my bedroom. Seeing, smelling, touching and hearing Nature in your home.

When I accepted my relationship with Nature and the responsibility that came with it, including that of the spiritual realm, I grew at alarming pace. Each time I returned to Jamaica after my furlough experience, I conquered what little fear I had at that time. Most often I walked in the dark and by myself (normally after my work day while the days were growing shorter as well). I would walk a bit further on my path each day until I passed through a fallen tree on the path just before reaching the place of my initial vision. Passing the fallen tree, symbolized a breakthrough moment. No more fear.

Throughout my life, now at age sixty-seven, I have incorporated many ritual aspects into my ceremony and/or validated their importance/relevance by their existence in other religions. Most of us have seen how candles, incense, prayer, chanting, bells and chimes, musical instruments play a role in church ceremony. Holding hands in prayer creates unity and makes ceremony more spiritually rewarding. It brings a greater flow of spiritual energy if shared. No where better than the power of words used in prayers. A mantra repeated again and again. Better yet, a mantra that you manifested and can relate to the meaning behind them. I had my own mantra, a powerful and meaningful name that was inscribed on my walking stick before it was painted and hidden. I often spread tobacco around the perimeter of my cabin before ceremony. Most importantly, every action is sacred in ceremony.

Smudging is used in energy clearing work, healing and ceremonies. Smudging involves burning herbs in either a red abalone shell or from the common smudge stick string bundles.

The sage and cedar are used to cleanse and protect a person's aura and their sacred surroundings. While, the sweet grass might be burned afterwards to welcome in positive energy, peace and love into the sacred space. Different cultures, tribes or individual preferences will dictate how one goes about this same ritual. Usually a meditation or prayer precedes or continues during the cleansing. I open with a prayer and focus on the cleansing task at hand in a spiritual way.

For individuals, a cleansing can begin at either the feet or head or heart of the person. When smudging myself, I prefer to start at the feet, up and down each leg to the waist and up and down each arm the chest and circle above the head at least twice - the crown chakra. When smudging someone else I do the same and also repeat the process down their back side.

For sacred places such as my cave, my cabin and home. Smudging can begin at the east wall, west wall, or a front entrance. Performed either clockwise or counter clockwise. Normally a door should be open to allow the negative energies to escape. Upon researching this process, I found that some Native American tribes recommended starting in the direction of the east. Upon reflection, I always smudged from the east side counter clockwise in my cave, cabin and home, not planned or intended. I smudge extensively across the walls, closets, bath and shower and paying even more attention to the perimeter of the windows and doors where energies can enter our space. Very rarely would I follow with sweet grass. I often watched the swirling smoke rise as I smudged along. It is ceremony and reminds me of such ceremony I have seen in church where you see the energy interacting with the air, flowing upwards with any intended message you wish to send. I go about it in a spiritual way.

Somewhere I learned a meditation involving five postures that align my chakras and connect myself with the surrounding energies. I would usually follow with prayer. My crown chakra always opens. I have performed these movements, in my home, in my cabin and in Nature. I can feel a strong etheric connection in any one of these places but I see more energy while in Nature's presence. My postures begin with me standing up right. #1 Both of my arms are extended in front of me, palms down. I lift both arms above my head but remaining in front of me, my hands dropping from my wrists, my arms stopping waist high. This motion can be repeated as often as you are comfortable. I generally, do it once and move on to the next posture. #2 Raise and bend your arms back to your shoulders, palms facing away from you, turn each arm away from you to your respective side, left towards the left, right towards the right, and eventually stretch each arm out, palms remain facing away from you. Bring arms in towards respective breast with palms facing in, turn palms down towards ground and let your arms down as far as they go, remaining upright. #3 Bring arms up and across your chest, forming an x, palms facing in, bring right arm out to side with arm curled up and palm facing you. Repeat the same with your left arm by bringing left arm out to side with arm curled down and palm facing you, bring arms in again and across your chest, forming an x, repeat same posture with opposite arms out curled out again but right is downward and left is upward. bring arms to chest again, meeting palms in middle and let arms drop down in front of you with palms down #5 bring each arm up extended to form a circle above your head, bring arms down as is in front of you, fingers facing in towards each other and arms

how I developed a relationship with nature

eventually straightening out as they fall in front of you with palms facing down. If there is a posture I repeat, it is generally this one. This posture opens my crown chakra. What variations work best for you, slow or slower, eyes open or eyes shut. Recently, I have only used a few postures, very very slow, and very deliberate. Resulting in same comforting and soothing feelings, if not more. I am often facing my mantel towards the direction of the East.

To provide a quick synopsis of chakras, I refer to Barbara Ann Brennan in her book, Hands of light. She describes the seven major chakras as the base, sacral, solar plexus, heart, throat, forehead and crown chakras. Energy is transmitted from one layer to the next progressive layer, the crown being the highest located any where from three and half feet above our head. Each of these vortices bring the development of different aspects of self-consciousness (ie. etheric, mental, emotional, spiritual) and exchange energy with the universal energy field. I was pleased to validate my own experiences, some as simple as feeling the energy on my finger tips to more profoundly feeling my crown chakra.

Concentrate on the chakras. Understand and learn the chakra energies about yourself and you present an opportunity to merge them with Nature's energies.

It was about this same time that a spiritual teacher taught me about protecting myself with white light if I felt a negative presence coming my way. I take my right hand (I'm right handed) and simply wand my front side of my body, palm facing in, saying "white light".

My first meditations took place at home. You often hear people say close your eyes, relax, breath deeply, call white light into you, visualize buckets of clean water, clear water replacing the old water. Emptying to make room for the clean, clear water. Rhythmic breathing, fresh cool air inhaled replenishing your body, warm stale air exhaled from within you.

My first few times I meditated on my couch late evenings following some light reading and hot tea. The lights are out, the shades are drawn and the candles are burning. The telephone ringer is off. A drumming tape plays at times. Quiet, relaxed and at peace, I lie face up on the couch, my palms up, and arms by my side. Facing East and at times, West. Covered with a blanket and my staff placed diagonally across my body. I focus on my breath and repeat my mantra. I usually feel tingling throughout my body, an extension of my body at times as though my energy was spreading out from me. The warmth and energy flows into my palms continuously. My body was in a rhythm. My head would toss gently and effortlessly.

Meditations follow and I begin to ask questions.

The first time I asked the spiritual world if I could come to them. I had always welcomed them into my life, into my world. Now I felt comfortable coming to them. I remember feeling a tap or nudge to the side of stomach as if someone wanted to let me know they were here. I continued to feel much tingling throughout my body. A lift in the energy around me. A white aura around me.

On two separate experiences, I heard chanting of elders from above and far away to what seem to be in front of me. I could not make out the words, native chant. I could hear my heart beat. I could feel my heart beat. I could hear the silence in between. The chanting and the beating of drum (heart beat). The message conveyed to me was to understand myself and to teach others the value of understanding themselves and being outdoors.

One time, I saw an eagle face at the foot of my couch, and another time, a Native American face, who validated their presence through their yellow eyes. Another message, continue to follow your path. And one of my most common answers I would hear, "the answer will come in time."

I became comfortable meditating in Nature, in particular, standing in the natural strong sun light, blinding and warm. I focused on the sun light running down from my head (crown chakra) through my body (other chakras) into the ground. I would see variations of color - purple, blue, and green and ending with yellow, orange, and red. They appeared simultaneously, not separately. Perhaps the chakras were opening simultaneously or one right after the other and the energies flowing rather quickly. I would feel recharged.

Another time sitting on Mother Earth, I focus on my breath, repeat my mantra, and perform my meditative postures. I feel my energy running, the blood flowing through my body. I could feel the energy around my head, soothing, goose bumps coming and going, a buzzing sound as well.

My time spent at the cave (Chapter 8) illustrate just how special this cave and its surrounding lands were to my personal and spiritual development. "When they have a difficult problem to deal with, they climb the mountain to clear their heads and make a final decision on the summit, where the stiff breeze and the wonderful view seem somehow to make it easier." (40)

My meditation here was more ceremonial in Nature. I always smudged myself and the nearby crevices of the cave. I gaze out at the forest canopy and valley below before lying upon my woven blanket and a bed of leaves. Facing South (the direction of growth and expansion) and East (the direction of clear vision, awareness, enlightenment, and new beginnings). I now look up at the sky and the ceiling of the cave and begin to appreciate those who came here before me. I often recite my Nature prayer and chanted my mantra. I was very at peace, feeling very much a part of where I was, feeling the energy and connection around me. I would stay here for hours and would leave only out of necessity. I often experienced a sense of lightness, moving effortlessly, floating steps, my muscles relaxed, an expanded mind and body, and a very heightened awareness and closeness to the forest here. I could feel my heart beat slowly beating, not pounding. While climbing out of the mountain, my gratitude for the experience overcomes any disappointment about returning to society. This was truly my special place to connect to the natural and spiritual world.

My cabin became my go to place to replace my cave and home.

I spoke earlier of a few of my meditation/prayers at the cabin while sitting in my rocking chair. Meditations here, began with my postures, followed by my set of prayers, and my focus towards the north facing walls (the direction of wisdom and insight) and the Ojibway traditional design shield. (described earlier as a round shield representing the eagle society of the Ojibway tribe, half red/ half dark blue with the eagle centered half blue/ half white respectively, turkey feathers attached, hang below it. Representing war and peace). Sometimes, I swiveled in my chair and faced the wooden eagle on the window sill, facing East. Meditation now comes easy.

Initially, all of my meditations were conducted in a ceremonial way. First the candles, the smoke….Now, I sit or lie in a quiet place, relax and meditate and pray. It has always come naturally where ever and when ever. Generally it occurred during my evenings up until I retired a few years ago. Now more daytime, facing West in my chair and facing East while lying down in my bed. Recently, I have found my hands clasped and my fingers interlocked together. My thumbs forming a cross and my index fingers forming a steeple. It reminds me of the nursery rhyme cited by my Mom that goes a bit like this "here is the church, here is the steeple, open the door, here are all of the people." Thank you Mom.

When I began developing relationships with many animals, I wanted to learn everything about them. I read many books about their habitat and behavior. I came across the word totem in my readings. "I believe that the term totem originated as a natural object or animal adopted as a name for Native American tribes and clans. It was an animal to whose energy they felt closely associated with during their lives. If we honor a totem, we also honor the essence behind it. Their energies empower and protect us and can help us to heal and grow. Shamans work to reconnect conscious human life with Nature and spirit through animal totems". (41)

The staff is a symbol of the tree of life, the axis between heaven

how I developed a relationship with nature

and earth. It is a tool to take messages skyward. It provides support, and it gives direction and intensity to energy. The staff is a symbol of the link to your most spiritual energies.

One evening while reading about the observation of energy or auras and ability to draw energy from an object or send energy to one. It specifically mentioned a walking stick or staff were good power objects. Ted Andrews suggested decorating it, "painting it with colors symbolic and significant to your purpose. You may wish to use some of ancient alphabets and carve names and words important to you and your life goals…. Each time I use it, it becomes more charged, and it becomes easier to access the energies."(41)

I went to my car and grabbed my walking staff out of my trunk and returned to my candle lit room. I had already painted and carried it in many places and ceremonies as suggested in this reading. I had painted relative colors and inscribed it with special words and meanings. A turkey feather later tied to its top.

I experimented as I grasped my staff with both hands shoulder width apart and concentrated on sending energy from me through the center of my body up through my arms into the staff. I would grasp it tightly as I did this. After a few minutes, I was able to see like hairs off of the staff, surrounding the entire staff. I continued and I saw a white flame in between my clasped hands. I slept with the staff close to my chest that evening.

Again, another evening, I held my staff so gently, my right hand under it, the left holding over it, slowly rotating it one way, then the other way. I see the hair like projections and one strand of smoke, no flame. A few more evenings, I witness the hair like projections along edges of the staff as I send energy to it. I yawn at times. Whenever I take energy from it, I feel immensely strong.

The staff will and did accompany me to the cave and evening hikes. It is a part and extension of myself. It brings comfort and support while I'm in the woods and mountains.

My staff later helped me out on the long trail after I had fallen down the back side of Camels Hump. I was sliding down when I was able to catch my foot in a ridge. I was scared, I saw death and I could not bring myself to walk further down the path. Instead, I retreated and climbed back up on all fours and switch backed to my original path. I came upon what appeared to be a long haired Native American man (real life) as I crossed a nearby road way before I would enter the forest again. He says nice staff, it helps with balance. He shakes my hand in a congratulatory firm long hand shake and while looking into my eyes before walking away. The next 24 hours before reaching my car were very tiring. Long and short of it, I felt as though I was throttling back energy from my staff.

A bible verse, Psalms 23 for you, it references the historical importance of the staff, you have likely heard it before, "Yea, though I walk through the valley of the shadow of death, I will fear no evil: for thou art with me; thy rod and thy staff they comfort me."

Music and Dancing help us relax. In evenings, I would dance in front of woodstove, feeling the energy run thru the chakras and crown chakra. A ceremony of joy? Listening to the drumming and flute during meditation many years ago, now learning to play the flute.

Many years ago, I witnessed a long Native American prayer. He prayed for everything, the two leggeds, the four leggeds, winged creatures, the elements……. I learned that no prayer can be too long. Generally, When I say prayers to myself they can be long as well. They will begin with my thankfulness for the day and blessing everyone and end with my prayer below. Postures precede my prayer.

My original version of my Nature prayer. My second revision. My final revision. My prayer and its many revisions to meet my growing understanding and appreciation. Fine tune your prayer to meet your needs and strengthen their effect in the moment.

We call in the East Wind. The direction of spirit (and its totem, the eagle). To bring greater power to our prayers and intentions. To provide us with clear vision and awareness, new beginnings and enlightenment. We thank you.

how I developed a relationship with nature

We call in the South Wind (and its totem the deer). The direction of growth and expansion. Give us the strength to love and learn, love and learn, love and learn. Give us the strength to heal. Give us the strength to heal. Give us the strength to heal. We thank you. Thank you for live's gentle lessons.

We call in the West Wind (and its totem the mountain lion). Allow us to look within ourselves. To find harmony and balance. To find harmony and balance in all aspects of our lives. To find harmony and balance in our physical, mental, emotional, and spiritual lives. To find harmony and balance in our personal, family, community, church, love, work and play lives. We thank you.

We call in the North Wind (and its totem the bear). May your wisdom bring us insight. Show us how to understand our knowledge, how to use our knowledge, and the consequences of our knowledge. Show us how to be honest with ourselves. Show us how to be honest with others. Show us the truth. Show us the truth. Show us the truth. We thank you,

Grandfather Sun Thank you for your warmth and strength.

Grandmother moon Thank you for your changing faces and influences upon us. You make our lives so interesting.

Mother earth. We thank you for your many gifts. Please continue to provide us with your energies which will strengthen our connection to everything around you. We thank you.

We call on the Almighty Spirit, Sky Spirit, God and………..

Please protect, preserve and replenish our natural resources. Our Sky and air. Our Sun. Our waters. Our Earth. Please protect the habitat of the four leggeds, the two leggeds, the winged creatures, the finned creatures, the appendage free creatures, all creatures large and small. Please protect and replenish the mountains and the valleys, the forests, the grasslands, the deserts, the beaches, the marshes. All waters, the oceans, the rivers, lakes and ponds, the mountain brooks and streams, and the vernal pools. All habitat. All species. We thank you.

Prayer to me is one of my most powerful ways to enhance my relationship with Nature. Where everything is sacred and every action is sacred. Acknowledging the sacred, awakens the sacred. We remember that all things are related.

Peace within.

Chapter 11

The Call from the Spirits

It always seems to come back to the eagles. I have only shared this spiritual experience with a select few.

It was a time in my late thirties when I had the time to walk or kayak almost everyday. I was driven to be outdoors whenever I could find the time, beginning of the day, end of the day, mid day, all day. I could often be found walking at Jamaica State park or kayaking on local or far away waters in Vermont and New Hampshire. I had accepted the responsibility to grow spiritually and to stay grounded and very spiritual at this time in my life. It all began on the evening before my fortieth birthday.

My home had become my sacred space. My living room was spacious and it opened up to my game room which had a large Brunswick pool table at the time. My living room had a large oak mantel with oak pillars around my fireplace. A large blue ceramic wood stove was inserted to the fireplace. Its heat if not closely regulated could chase you out of both rooms. Many spectacular flames could be seen through the wood stove windows. Long time furniture in the room included, a fifteen year old enormous Pennsylvania couch below the front window. A coffee table in the center of the room. A tan corduroy chair by the center brick chimney.

Hanging ivy plants across the ceiling, divided the living room and game room. More hanging plants, one above an oak end table in the corner and a few above the couch. Wind chimes in each corner of these adjacent rooms.

All of the directions were represented in these rooms as well. Poster size pictures of wolves and a bear on the north facing wall, eagle figurines on the east facing mantle, a poster size picture a deer facing south, and a similar size mountain lion picture on the west wall.

I was often found sitting and laying on the couch at the end of the day with my woven blanket. Generally, facing East, sometimes West. The recessed ceiling lights were either dim or off and only the flames from the wood stove and a candle burning on the coffee table lit the room.

Occasional Native American drumming and flute music from a cassette player.

At times, my walking staff lay either on the floor beside me or across my chest as I lay on the couch.

House smudged, I'm smudged.

Relaxed.

A cup of my favorite chai or chamoille tea.

Reciting my mantra.

Watching flames in the wood stove and candle.

how I developed a relationship with nature

My ears ringing.

A very ceremonial setting. A peaceful place.

The morning of November 3, 1997 at approximately 3AM one day before my 40th birthday. I had planned to spend my 40th birthday possibly camping out by myself, however, today, in a few hours I would be leaving for facilitator training for one week, far removed from any outdoors adventure.

Earlier in the evening, perhaps close to midnight, I felt an intense pulling from my chest to go outdoors to one of my favorite walks. I was lying on the couch, facing the window. A force pulling at me. Urging me. Accept it and respond to it. I did not. The pull was so strong that I felt pulled up against the back side of the couch. There seemed little I could do. I fought it, resisted it best I can, saying that I'll drive back home tomorrow and go there for an evening walk. Later that evening, I felt my chest pullout. I remember tossing over and over most of the evening, finding it difficult to sleep. Laying on one side, looking out the window, I remember seeing the starry sky, later a cloudy one, then a starry sky. Clouds, stars, clouds, stars, tossing, turning, tossing, turning.

Later, I found myself lying face down on the couch, my arms grasping the pillow under my head. Suddenly, I'm doing the same in an open field of grass atop a mountain, overlooking a valley with trees on each side, and an eagle which is above trees to the left at a great distance away, however, bigger and coming closer. I could hear it hovering above me. All I could say was WOW, WOW, WOW. I kept arching my back up to see more. I wanted more of it. I felt warmth and an infusion of energy into my shoulders, moving down towards my chest to my stomach. It last more than a few seconds. I remember a lot of movement and tossing throughout the night. Lots of stars. And the sound of the river and wings.

Happy birthday. Home alone on your fortieth birthday. The next morning, my back and lower back actually ached from arching it that evening. A previous tender and sore bicep was completely healed as well. What happened? A vivid dream? A real or imagined spiritual experience?

I didn't always know exactly what these events meant at the time but felt blessed by them. I felt an even stronger spiritual connection with the eagles. My relationship heartened. I was welcomed into their world, more specifically, their spiritual realm. ' Eagles say do you want to learn how to fly ? See the great creation through my eyes? Dance on the wind as I do? (42). It was a joyful experience for me.

I have been blessed by more spiritual encounters but not relative to our conversation about developing our relationship with Nature. I will say that I have recently had a revelation, one early morning in February of last year. I was to begin writing a new book called "Being Thankful". Some sub titles were provided to me and more spiritual encounters to be included as well. I am very excited because a similar revelation occurred many many years ago when I began writing "Peace Within". I have begun to read more books and note my own thoughts and experiences preparing to write "Being Thankful". This upcoming book might be for public distribution or a personal memoir for family and friends.

Please read on to "Blessings" and my "Heartfelt Conclusion."

Peace within.

Chapter 12

Counting My Blessings

My spiritual relationship with Nature has blessed my life in many ways. A spiritual presence remains constant during my changing times - good relationships, bad, and in different. I become increasingly aware of the energy abound and the spiritual realm .

I become aware of how my body, mind, and spirit are interrelated. I am aware of my own energy around my body, my aura. I learned a Tibetan movement that allowed me to feel and align my energies/chakras.

It did not take long before I developed a relationship with my higher and spiritual self. I accepted the presence of spirit in my life and the responsibility that came with it and it grew even stronger.

I begin to trust myself, my spiritual side, my inner guidance. More trust, less worry, less fear. I have a true sense of what is really important? Enjoying each moment. Everything flowing at times.

As I grow, I learn more and appreciate more. Understanding increases yet more questions follow. Constantly learning more.

Be in the moment, appreciate what I have in the moment. Have faith and trust in yourself and your life, most importantly spiritually.

Spirit guides, totems protect me, especially in Nature and my home.

I feel the spiritual presence in my life. Most recently, a spiritual teacher just letting me know that they are here, watching over me and here to comfort me. One late evening, I awaken to a tall female spiritual presence at the foot of my bed. Surprised, I white light myself. A former deceased spiritual teacher letting me know that I am not alone. A comforted tingling on my entire back side as our auras merge. Best described as a tingling sensation like the sparkling sunlight reflecting on quiet lake waters.

I see auras around others, particularly those in religious or ceremonial settings. I see the golden aura of priests and ministers, clergy. I attended mass at a monastery many years ago. The eyes of the monks were intense, bright and enlightened. They seem at peace. Some, I observed a glow. The head monk definitely had a white aura surrounding his entire head down to the neck. The room seemed bright. People of the congregation swayed back and forth as they sang.

I continue to see more auras usually ones at the pulpit in church. At times, a pastor's aura from her head and shoulders down to as far as I can see from my view.

I feel the merging of my aura with another occasionally when meeting someone spiritually aroused in an emotional, innocent way.

I see angels in my home and church. Again, comforting me, letting me know that they are watching over loved ones. While sitting on my couch one evening, our cat sensed a presence across the room and my eyes followed a waist high presence from my dining room into my daughters room, I believe to be a child size guardian angel at the time.

how I developed a relationship with nature

I had visions, short ones and long ones, usually relative to my life circumstances at the time and my relationship with Nature and others. They also addressed the element of overcoming fear based thoughts in my life and allowing me to grow and appreciate new experiences in my life.

"The answers will come in time" were often the responses to my questions.

I was willing to learn and explore new things in my life. I read as many as two hundred books and experimented with forms of meditation and shamanic journeys.

I attended several shamanic workshops, read about them and eventually led a few of them.

Some twenty-five years ago, I was comfortable being called a shaman by some of my spiritual teachers and closer friends. Shaman love silence. Everything in Nature flows into him and from him. A shaman has finely tuned perceptions able to pick up things with their senses. So to this day, I still maintain my personality and traits of a shaman even though I do not consider myself an active, practicing shaman at this time. I continue to meditate and pray in my home and in Nature.

To appreciate and respect all religions and their ceremonies. Incense, ringing of bells, candles, chanting, singing, praying . I respect other people where others might be in their lives, how they are feeling and the roles they are playing in my life and others lives.

To love and learn. Living and speaking from the heart but also practicing the principle of noninterference. I had it repeated to me many times before, "the answer will come in time". Although, I might have an answer or guidance to provide another, more often than not, that person has to be willing and able to hear and understand the answer.

To say my prayers, both religious and Nature - both spiritual, both enhance my life. Seeing angels. Animals suddenly appearing. Why would I not say prayers. I am blessed to see them. Why would I not pray for them. Why would I not be thankful for seeing them, hearing them, communicating with them. If I believe my prayers are not answered, I say them more for I am thankful for them, always. I always thank them for listening. Who do I thank? Who do you thank?

I recognize that I (we) can always improve upon our prayers and recite them more often. I improve upon my prayers more and more to this day as I continue to meditate and pray.

My life's perspective changed as well. I reclaimed my childlike wonder -as if I am seeing things for the first time. I catch leaves in the wind just as I did as a child. I enjoy and appreciate the moment.

To teach and share my thoughts and experiences in this book.

To always do the right thing as difficult as it might be for myself and others in that moment. Speak up for " the greater good" and be a positive voice when witnessing the mistreatment of our children, our elderly, our challenged, and our environment.

Most importantly, to learn as elders that all relationships are all related. Truth -deep love and awareness of man's inter-relationship to all things in Nature.

Peace Within.

My Heartfelt Conclusion

I trust you will form a relationship with Nature and recognize the importance of Mother Earth, its elements, its animals, its energy in our lives. I have sited many spiritual experiences all made possible by my relationship with Nature. Native American elders have taught us that all things are related. Our relationship with Nature and spirits, friends and family, and others are the most important things in our lives.

I'll share with you my favorite Nature prayer that I often recite after my "calling in the directions." The prayer asks for the protection of the habitat of all living things. It begins,

Mother Earth, Almighty Spirit,

Please protect the habitat of all our relations, the four leggeds, the two leggeds, large and small, our winged creatures in the sky, our finned creatures in the waters, appendige-free creatures everywhere, all species and their habitats, Please protect our earth, its mountains, the valleys, our forests, meadows, and edge. The deserts. The air, our sun and sky. Our waters, brooks and streams, lakes and ponds, rivers and oceans...........

It is imperative that all of us understand that we are all related and interconnected with Nature. It will only be when we all truly care about our Mother Earth and make changes in our lives to conserve, preserve and protect our natural environment.

Please continue to "love and learn" and share our knowledge, understanding and love of Nature with our children and loved ones.

Weeks before beginning my publication process, I came across this passage that I would like to share with you.

"DO NOT DOUBT WHAT YOU SEE. Last night they came again, the spirits of earth and sky, of wind and rain, of deep seas and tall mountains. In all shapes and sizes they came, from every tribe and nation: the deer and elk, the bear and wolf, broad-winged eagles and crows as black as night. They all came and stood in a solemn circle beneath the one-eyed moon and spoke with a single voice this message from the sacred: Do not doubt what you see: the world is warming, the waters are rising and the winds are coming stronger than before. Do not turn away, do not pretend not to see, but speak the truth and set the spirits free to heal the world, before the ice is gone, before the last tiger falls, before only the desert remembers the ones who once walked this land." (43)

A portion of the proceeds from this book will be donated to The Nature Conservancy, a global environmental nonprofit organization working to create a world where people and Nature can thrive together. It's mission to conserve the lands and waters on which all life depends.

    Peace within,

      John

Recommended Readings

Andrews, Ted **Animal-Speak**, Llewellyn Publications 1997

Archie Fire Lame Deer & Richard Erdoes **Gift Of Power**, Bear & Company 1992

Bear Heart with Molly Larkin **The Wind Is My Mother**, Berkley Books 1998

Braden, Gregg **Walking Between The Worlds**, Radio Bookstore 1997

Brennan Barbara Ann **Hands Of Light**, Bantam Books 1988

Brown, Joseph Epes **The Spiritual Legacy Of The American Indian**, World Wisdom Inc 2007

Buhlman, William **Adventures Beyond The Body**, Harper Collins 1996

Cohen, Kenneth **Honoring The Medicine**, Ballantine Books 2003

Dolfyn **Shamanic Wisdom**, Earthspirit Inc. 1990

Dreaver, Jim **The Way Of Harmony**, Avon Books Inc. 1999

Garrett, Michael **Walking On The Wind**, Bear & Company 1998

Garrett, J.T. & Michael Garrett **Medicine Of The Cherokee**, Bear & Company 1996

Hull, Michael **Sun Dancing**, Inner Traditions International 2000

Jones, Robert Blackwolf, M.S.,C.A.S, Gina Jones **Listen To The Drum**, Hazelden Foundation 1995

Kabat-Zinn, Jon **Wherever You Go There You Are**, Hyperion 1994

Kavasch, E. Barrie & Karen Baar **American Indian Healing Arts**, Bantum Books 1999

Kelder, Peter **Foundation Of Youth**, Harbor Press Inc 1998

Linn, Denise **Sacred Space**, Ballantine Books 1995

Mariechild, Diane **Mother Wit**, The Crossing Press 1981

Mathews, John **The Celtic Shaman**, Element Books Ltd 1991

McGaa, Ed Eagle Man **Nature's Way**, Harper Collins 2004

Meadows, Kenneth **Where Eagles Fly,** Element Books Ltd 1995

Prather, Hugh & Gayle **Spiritual Parenting**, Harmony Books 1996

Prophet, Mark L. & Elizabeth Clare **Climb The Highest Mountain**, Summit University Press 1986

Rael, Joseph with Mary Elisabeth Marlow **Being & Vibration**, Council Oak Brooks 1993

Redfield, James **The Celestine Vision**, Warner Books Inc. 1997

Rezendes, Paul **The Wild Within**, Berkley Book 1998

Roman, Sanaya **Spiritual Growth**, H.J. Kramer Inc 1989

Royal, Lyssa **Millennium**, Royal Priest Research Press 1998

Scott PH.D, Gini Graham **Shamanism & Personal Mastery**, Paragon House 1991

Snellgrove, Brian **The Unseen Self**, C.W. Daniel Co Ltd. 1996

Steiger, Brad **Indian Medicine Power**, Whitford Press 1984

Sun Bear, Crysalis Mulligan, Peter Nafer & Wabun **Walk In Balance**, Fireside Book 1989

Tooker, Elisabeth **Native North American Spirituality Of The Eastern Woodlands**, Paulist Press 1979

Wolfe, Amber **In The Shadow Of The Shaman**, Llewellyn Publications 1999

Bibliography

Andrews, Ted   Animal Speaks. The Spiritual & Magical Powers of Creatures Great & Small.   Llewellyn Publications 1997 2143 Woodpile Drive, Woodbury, MN. 55125-2989 Permission granted. Quoted pages 256, 50, 262,126, 136-141, 29, 63, 113, and 8. Respective footnotes 9, 11, 12, 16, 17, 18, 20, 24, 34,41.

Bear, Luther Standing My People the Sioux, University of Nebraska Press. 2006 Quoted pages 268-269. Contact address UNPrights@unl.edu Respective footnote 14.

Brandon, Craig Monadnock More Than A Mountain. Surry Cottage Books 2007 25 Roxbury Street, Keene, NH. 03431 Fair Use. Quoted from pages 19, 20, 26,151.Respective footnote 33, 35, 39, 40.

Brennan, Barbara Ann   The Hands of Light. A Guide to Healing Through the Human Energy Field. Bantam Books 1988 666 5th Avenue, New York, New York 10103 Contact address permissions@Penguinrandomhouse.com No formal permission required, considered Fair Use. Referenced pages 44, 72-79. Respective footnotes 25, 27.

Brown, Tom Jr.   Grandfather, The Berkley Publishing Group 1993 The Berkley Publishing Group, a division of Penguin Putnam Inc., 375 Hudson Street, New York, New York 10014 contact address permissions@Penguinrandomhouse.com Permission granted Fair use. Quoted pages 73-74. Respective footnote 2.

Charlestown, Steven   Ladder to the Light. An Indigenous Elder's Meditations on Hope And Courage, Broadleaf Books 2021 PO Box

1209, Minneapolis, MN. 55440-1209 Permission granted. Quoted from page 131. Respective footnote 43.

Fagen, Brian The First North Americans an Archeological Journey, Thames & Hudson 2011 500 Fifth Avenue, New York, New York 10110 Fair Use. Quoted page 51. Respective footnote 1.

Garrett, J.T. & Michael Garrett Ph.D. Medicine of the Cherokee. The Way of Right Relationship., published by Inner Traditions International and Bear & Company. 1996 All rights reserved. http://www.Innertraditions.com Reprinted with permission of publisher. Quoted from page 217. Respective footnotes 21, 42.

Jones, Blackwood & Gina Jones Listen To The Drum. Blackwood Shares His Medicine., Hazelden Foundation 1995 copyrightpermissions@hazeldenbettyford.org no longer represent copy right. Unable to contact authors. Fair Use. Referenced from pages 111, 112, and 115. Respective footnote 37.

Linn, Denise Sacred Space. Clearing and Enhancing the Energy of your Home., Ballantine Books 1995 A Division of Random House Inc., 1745 Broadway, New York, New York 10019 Permission granted Fair use. Quoted from pages 247,248. Respective footnote 23.

Long, William How Animals Talk, Published by Inner Traditions International and Bear & Company, 1919, 2005. All rights reserved. http://www.Innertraditions.com Reprinted with permission of publisher. Quoted pages 47-49 & 188, 150. Respective footnotes 15, 19, 31.

Marshall III, Joseph M. The Lakota Way. Stories and lessons for living., Penguin Group 2001, 375 Hudson Street, New York, New York 10014 Contact address Permissions@penguin randomhouse.com Permission granted Fair use. Quoted from page 197. Respective footnote 7.

Olsen, Andrea Body and Earth. An Experimental Guide., University Press of New England 2002 One Court Street, Lebanon, NH 03766 Fair use. Quoted page 226. Respective footnote 13.

Redfield, James The Celestine Vision., Warner Books Inc. 1997 1271 Avenue of the Americas, New York, New York 10020 Fair Use. Quoted from page 99. Respective footnote 36.

Russell, Howard S. Indian New England Before the Mayflower, University Press of New England 1980 One Court Street, Lebanon, NH. 03766 Now Wesleyan University Permissions Website. Fair use. Quoted from pages 100, 43-44. Respective footnotes 6 and 8.

Suzuki, David Excerpt from The Sacred Balance Rediscovering Our Place in Nature (25th Anniversary Edition) by David Suzuki with Amanda McConnell and Adrienne Mason. Reprinted with permission from Greystone Books, 343 Railway Street, Suite 302, Vancouver, British Columbia, Canada V6A 1A4. rights@greystonebooks.com Permission granted. Quoted from pages 268-269. Respective footnotes 10, 22.

Van Etten, Jaap PHD Gifts of Mother Earth. Earth Energies, Vortexes, Lines, And Grids 3 Light Technology Publishing LLC 2011 PO Box 3540, Flagstaff, AZ 86003 contact address publishing@lighttechnology.com Permission granted. Quoted pages 10-14, 24-25, 131 & 191, 19, Respective footnotes 3, 4, 5, 26, 28, 29, 32, 38.

www.umrich.edu Mother Earth Fair use. Respective footnote 30.

Every attempt has been made to trace accurate ownership of copyrighted material in this book. Errors and omissions will be corrected in subsequent editions provided that notification is sent to the publisher.

About the Author

Hello I'm John. I have been called a Shaman by a few of my spiritual teachers many many years ago, a Buddha by some many years ago, a Deacon by many in recent years, a Nature loving person and more importantly dad throughout most of my life. Although, I am not Native American and not a practicing Shaman, I would call myself a deeply religious and spiritual man starting with my strong connection with Nature. I am an every day person, confronted with the same issues, more or less, as you are everyday. I worked forty hours a week. I am twice divorced. I have two older adult children, John and Katherine and my younger son, Kaden. I once lived from pay check to pay check. ......

  I do enjoy my life and the outdoors in a very special way. More than twenty-five years ago, I began documenting my experiences in Nature, with the notion that I would someday be writing a book. I have also read close to two hundred books on the subject of Nature and spirituality. I have always believed that if I learn one thing from a book or article, my reading was time well spent. This book is a collection of my very personal, truth telling experiences, my interpretations, and wisdom. My goal is to provide you with the same opportunities and validate some of your own similar experiences.

What happened to me? When I was a child I played in Nature all of the time. I walked barefoot on the beach, playing in the waves, collecting shells and sand dollars ...I tried to catch leaves in the wind, jumped into piles of leaves, climbing trees... I tried catching snow flakes, sledding down hills, making snow angels...I danced in the rain, splashed in the puddles, swimming...Catching butterflies, fireflies, frogs, poly-wogs...Skimming rocks on a pond.. . Smelling flowers.. Tasting wild berries.. Lay on the grass, looking up at the blue sky, at the many different clouds, admiring colors of a rainbow after a rain shower... Seeing things for the first time. It was always a new experience. I was lost in the moment.

As I went through adolescence, I spent more time in school and studies, sports, and relationships. Then on to college, more studies, partying and relationships. I graduated and moved from one job to another. As an adult I became distracted by modern day society and its technology- the responsibility of paying bills, watching television, reading newspapers, influenced by the aggressive advertising, the violence, focused upon relationship problems in my personal life and the work place. Fear based thoughts occupied my time. Who am I? Where am I going? Somewhere, I lost my childlike wonder.

In my early 30's I began spending more time outdoors. Recently divorced, two young children and more added responsibility than I ever imagined. I walked in nearby parks, hiked the Long Trail in Vermont, climbed mountains such as Mount Monadnock in New Hampshire, kayaked lakes and rivers in New England. Gradually, I began to reintegrate myself back into Nature and discover my own true nature. The beauty of silence and an opportunity to gather my thoughts. I began to grow. My relationship with Nature grew stronger and I was very comfortable wherever I was in Nature. And WOW, it finally reached a turning point, I allowed myself to experience the unusual. Beginning with the day of the furlough.